Oedipus at Colonus

Publication of this volume has been made possible in part

through the generous support and enduring vision of

Warren G. Moon.

Oedipus at Colonus

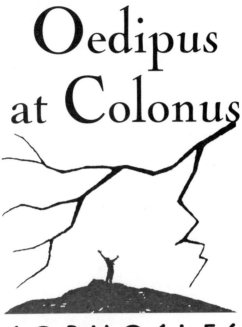

SOPHOCLES

A verse translation by
David Mulroy,
with introduction and notes

The University of Wisconsin Press

The University of Wisconsin Press
1930 Monroe Street, 3rd Floor
Madison, Wisconsin 53711-2059
uwpress.wisc.edu

3 Henrietta Street, Covent Garden
London WC2E 8LU, United Kingdom
eurospanbookstore.com

Printed in the United States of America

Library of Congress Cataloging-in-Publication Data

Sophocles, author.
[Oedipus at Colonus. English]
Oedipus at Colonus / Sophocles; a verse translation by David Mulroy,
with introduction and notes.
pages   cm—(Wisconsin studies in classics)
Includes bibliographical references.
ISBN 978-0-299-30254-2 (pbk.: alk. paper)
ISBN 978-0-299-30253-5 (e-book)
1. Oedipus (Greek mythology)—Drama.
I. Mulroy, David D., 1943– translator.
II. Title.   III. Series: Wisconsin studies in classics.
PA4414.O5M85   2014
882'.01—dc23
2014009155

For

Roy Swanson

Contents

Preface

Oedipus at Colonus is one of Sophocles' seven extant tragedies. He probably composed it shortly before his death in 406 or 405 BCE at the age of eighty-nine.[1] It was first produced posthumously in 401 BCE and may be viewed as the sequel to Sophocles' masterpiece, *Oedipus Rex*, which was probably written in the 420s.

Since *Oedipus at Colonus* is rarely the first Sophoclean tragedy that a reader tackles, I will forego summarizing Sophocles' life and times and the general characteristics of the ancient Greek theater. I have written on those topics in my other two translations of Sophoclean works, *Oedipus Rex* and *Antigone*.[2]

Many excellent translations of Sophocles' plays, including *Oedipus at Colonus*, have been published in recent years. My translations are distinguished by the lengths I go to in order to recapture something of the rhythmic and musical character of the original Greek productions. Specifically, I have translated the spoken parts of the original into regular iambic pentameters, whereas the lyrical passages are translated into short rhymed stanzas. The original Greek also contains some anapests and trochees, which I have imitated in English. In addition to telling good stories, Greek tragedies were full of auditory pleasures. I consider my translations successful to the extent that the same can be said of them. They are meant to be read aloud.

If I were assigning my *Oedipus at Colonus* in a high school or college course, I doubt that I would require my own introduction. Equipped with footnotes where meanings are obscure, the play is accessible on its own. For students with little previous knowledge of Greek literature, however, I would highly recommend the first part of that introduction, "The Story of *Oedipus at Colonus*," a summary of the play with excerpts from the dialogue. Its quick overview of the story will prepare them to read the whole play without getting lost in the details, and the poetic excerpts will give them some appreciation of the play's verbal pyrotechnics.

For some time I have been fascinated by the question of whether or not Sophocles depicts Oedipus as morally responsible for his mistakes. In my opinion, the text accommodates both interpretations. In my translation of *Oedipus Rex* I note my surprise that so many critics insist that Oedipus is unambiguously innocent. In the second part of my introduction, "Oedipus as Tragic Hero," I return to that issue and lay out a case against him in somewhat greater detail—including some original iambic pentameters.

In the next two sections, I investigate a pair of related questions that caught my interest as I worked on my translation. The first was whether Sophocles himself invented the story of Oedipus' arrival, death, and burial in Colonus. The arguments pro and con are complicated and (I think) ultimately indecisive. On balance, I argue that the essential action of the play is probably Sophocles' own invention—and a highly topical one. Shortly before he wrote the play, an assembly met in the temple of Poseidon at Colonus and temporarily dissolved Athenian democracy. If the title did not reflect a well-established tradition, it resonated with controversial and contemporary political associations: imagine *Oedipus at Tahrir Square*.

Suggested by that conclusion, the next part of my introduction attempts to depict the political backdrop of *Oedipus at*

Colonus as well as that of the nearly contemporaneous *Philoctetes*. The plays were written during a period of desperate political tumult in Athens, which surely weighed heavily on Sophocles' mind. There is, of course, no one-to-one correspondence between Sophocles' characters and real-life politicians. On the other hand, the general points that are made in his plays often had obvious application to real life at the time. In the case of *Philoctetes* and *Oedipus at Colonus*, the piteous plight of exiles and their potential value to their native cities was a theme of unmistakable relevance to late fifth-century Athenians.

The introduction ends with some remarks on the religious implications of the play and a thought about Sophocles' family life.

In doing my translation, I relied principally on the Lloyd-Jones text in the Loeb Library together with Jebb's text and commentary.[3]

Notes

1. The date of Sophocles' birth is not known. According to the anonymous biography transmitted with the texts of his plays, he was said to have been born in the archon year 495/494 BCE. I use 495 in calculating his age at various junctures. The Greek text of Sophocles' biography is printed in S. Radt, *Tragicorum Graecorum Fragmenta IV: Sophocles* (Göttingen: Vandenhoeck and Ruprecht, 1977), 29–40; for an English translation, see M. Lefkowitz, *The Lives of the Greek Poets* (Baltimore and London: Johns Hopkins University Press, 1981), 160–63.

2. Sophocles, *Oedipus Rex*, a verse translation by David Mulroy (Madison: University of Wisconsin Press, 2011); Sophocles, *Antigone*, a verse translation by David Mulroy (Madison: University of Wisconsin Press, 2013).

3. H. Lloyd-Jones, *Sophocles: Antigone, The Women of Trachis, Philoctetes, Oedipus at Colonus* (Cambridge, MA: Harvard University Press, 1998); R. C. Jebb, *Sophocles: Plays, Oedipus Coloneus* (London: Bristol Classical Press, 2004; reprint of Jebb's 1900 edition published by the Cambridge University Press).

Introduction

The Story of *Oedipus at Colonus*

Oedipus at Colonus presupposes knowledge of *Oedipus Rex*. As Sophocles tells that story, Oedipus was the son of Laius and Jocasta, king and queen of Thebes. The oracle of Delphi warned Laius that he was destined to die by his child's hand. Therefore he and Jocasta ordered a servant to expose baby Oedipus, but the servant gave the baby to a friend to pass along to foster parents instead. Those turned out to be the king and queen of Corinth, who raised Oedipus as their own.

As a young man, Oedipus visited the oracle, hoping to dispel a rumor that he was illegitimate. Instead, the oracle told him that he was destined to kill his father and marry his mother. Hence Oedipus decided to flee Corinth, his presumptive parents' home. He turned toward Thebes. On the road he met Laius coming in the opposite direction, quarreled with him over the right of way, and killed him and his servants. Proceeding to Thebes, he found it harassed by a monster, the Sphinx, who was cornering young men in the countryside, asking them a riddle, and killing them when they failed to answer it. Oedipus confronted the Sphinx and answered her riddle, causing the monster to kill herself. The people of Thebes made him king. He married the newly widowed Queen Jocasta.

Oedipus and Jocasta lived happily for a long time, raising two sons, Polyneices and Eteocles, and two daughters, Antigone and Ismene. Eventually, the gods ended their happiness. A plague descended on Thebes, and the oracle advised Oedipus that it could be stopped only by punishing Laius' murderer. Oedipus vowed to find him. His investigation is the subject of *Oedipus Rex*. He finally succeeded in identifying the guilty party: himself. At the same time, he learned that his wife and the mother of his children, Jocasta, was also his own mother. In his distress, he blinded himself and begged to be driven into exile. His brother-in-law, Creon, who assumed royal power in the wake of Oedipus' downfall, told him to await further guidance from the oracle before quitting Thebes.

Oedipus Rex ends on that note. *Oedipus at Colonus* picks up the story years later. Oedipus, a blind, exiled beggar, wanders Greece in the company of his daughter Antigone. They happen to stop in a pleasant grove in Colonus, a suburb of Athens. A local resident tells them that they must leave the grove, since it is sacred to the Eumenides (a.k.a. the Furies), the dread goddesses of the underworld. Oedipus refuses to move, saying that it is his fate to be in the grove. The resident's reply is surprisingly bland. He says that he will have to consult with his fellow townsmen and leaves to do so. Alone with Antigone, Oedipus prays to the Eumenides. As he does, we learn that he is destined to die in the grove (84–91):

> O goddesses of fearsome countenance,
> since I've approached your sanctuary first,
> treat me and lord Apollo graciously.
> When he foretold my many sufferings,
> he said I'd find this resting place in time,
> and it would mark my journey's end. He said
> that I'd be welcomed where great goddesses
> reside, and there I'd end my sorry life.

A chorus of local residents enters singing while Oedipus and Antigone hide in the bushes. Such a choral entrance is a regular feature of Greek tragedies. The song that the chorus sings as they enter is known as the *parodos*. Its subject always fits the chorus's fictional identity and its immediate, fictional concerns. In this instance, the chorus consists of local elders who are up in arms at hearing that a stranger has invaded the Eumenides' sacred grove (117–127):

> *Who was the man and where's he now?*
> *He's disappeared. We wonder how.*
> *The boldest man of all.*
>
> *He's surely wandered far and wide.*
> *No native son would step inside*
> *the grove of savage maids . . .*

After listening briefly, Oedipus discloses his location, speaking in anapests (138–139):

> Up here! I am he. It's by sound that I see—
> to speak in a figurative manner.

A heated exchange ensues. The chorus interrogates Oedipus, who is reluctant to reveal his identity. When he finally does so, the chorus is apoplectic. They have heard Oedipus' story and demand that he leave their country instantly. His mere presence is a terrible pollution.

Normally the passages following a choral song consist of iambs spoken by actors, an approximation of normal speech. Deviations take the form of passages known as *kommoi*, "lamentations," in which the actors as well as the chorus sing in lyric meters. *Oedipus at Colonus* is distinguished by a relatively large number of lamentations. Not all of them are literal laments:

any emotional exchange provides suitable material. A striking feature of the Greek lamentations is that changes of speaker (or singer) sometimes occur within a metrical unit (or a stanza, in our terms). Thus when the chorus urges Oedipus to leave the grove in which he has taken shelter and to sit on its periphery, we have sung exchanges like this (192–197):

> CHORUS: *That's far enough, don't step beyond*
> *the marble platform there.*
> OEDIPUS: *Like so?* CHORUS: *That's right.* OEDIPUS: *And may I sit?*
> CHORUS: *Yes, make that rock your chair.*

A few minutes later, Oedipus is reluctant to reveal his identity (210–214):

> OEDIPUS: *Don't ask me who I am!*
> *Don't question me in any way!*
> CHORUS: *Why not?* OEDIPUS: *A horrid fate.*
> CHORUS: *Do tell!* OEDIPUS: *O daughter, what to say?*

When Oedipus does reveal his name, prompting the chorus to demand that he leave the country, he fights back with an extended speech, reverting to the iambic meter. He dwells on Athens' reputation as a defender of the weak (258–263):

> What good does reputation do or fame,
> however fair, that simply drifts away?
> So what if people say that Athens is
> most reverent, that she and only she
> protects the lives of persecuted men.
> Where did that virtue go when I arrived?

Oedipus' rhetoric is not without effect (292–295):

> CHORAL LEADER: Your arguments have shaken me, I must
> admit, old sir. Your protestation had
> no lack of weighty words. I think it best
> to let our ruler sort these matters out.

The ruler in question is the legendary hero Theseus, who is currently in the city of Athens itself. Oedipus is happy to have his case settled by him but wonders whether Theseus will deign to appear. The chorus is certain that he will come as soon as he hears Oedipus' name. In fact, there is no logical way for Theseus to hear that name, since Oedipus has only now revealed it to the chorus in the lonely countryside. But this is Greek tragedy. Information gets around as needed (303–305):

> CHORAL LEADER: The road is long, and travelers like to talk
> of many things. Be brave, for once he hears
> the gossip, he'll set forth.

Sophocles is fond of implying that one character is about to enter and then bringing in a different one. In this instance, the anti-Theseus is a young woman riding a pony and wearing a broad-brimmed hat that briefly conceals her identity. Antigone finally recognizes her. It is her sister, Oedipus' other daughter, Ismene. There is an emotional reunion. Oedipus praises his daughters for always looking out for him. On the other hand, he says, his sons have been worthless (342–355):

> My daughters, those who should endure your toils
> luxuriate at home like tender girls,
> while you have shared my awful suffering
> instead. Why she'd [*indicating Antigone*] no sooner given up
> her baby food and gained a bit of strength
> than she became my fellow wanderer,
> an old man's guide. . . .
> . . . .
> And you, my child [*indicating Ismene*], made secret trips from Thebes
> to bring your father all the oracles
> that mentioned him.

In the present instance, Ismene has tracked her father down to advise him that his two sons are fighting over control of

Thebes. The younger, Eteocles, has seized the throne. The elder, Polyneices, has raised an army in southern Greece and hopes to storm Thebes. Meanwhile, oracles have predicted that Oedipus' aid will be sought by the combatants while he is still alive and even after death. Power, they say, depends on him. Consequently, Creon is on his way to bring Oedipus back home— more or less.

Creon's specific goal is to settle Oedipus on the periphery of Theban territory. He is acting on the belief that the physical remains of heroes lend strength to the land in which they are buried. Hence Creon does not want another, potentially hostile nation to have control of Oedipus' remains. On the other hand, Oedipus has been banished from Thebes because of patricide and incest. The Thebans are not willing to rescind that decree. In an odd compromise, Oedipus will live and eventually die in no man's land, close enough for Thebes to keep watch over his remains, but technically outside Theban territory.[1]

Oedipus declares that he will never comply with Creon's wishes. As for his sons, they did not do anything to prevent his exile or help him survive. He will not support either side. As far as he's concerned, neither one will ever gain control of Thebes.

Still awaiting Theseus, the choral leader tells Oedipus to go into the grove and pour libations to the dread goddesses to propitiate them for trespassing. Because Oedipus is physically incapable of doing this himself, Ismene volunteers to act on his behalf (507–509):

> I'll go. You stay and guard our father well,
> Antigone. One mustn't call the work
> we do for parents toil—although it is.

Theseus finally arrives. He listens to Oedipus' account of his situation and responds graciously, granting him asylum. Undeterred by the fact that his action may bring him into conflict with Creon, he is impressed by Oedipus' promise that possession of his remains will prove beneficial to Athens.

Theseus departs, assuring Oedipus that his safety is guaranteed. We later learn (888) that he has gone to the nearby altar of Poseidon to offer sacrifice instead of going all the way back to Athens.

The chorus bursts into a song warmly praising Colonus and Athens. It was apparently a favorite in antiquity. The story arose that Sophocles' sons once sought control of their father's estate on the basis of his alleged mental incompetence, and his successful defense consisted of his recitation of this song (668–678):

> Horse country here, Colonus, where
> the finest farms on earth are found,
> and nightingales who fill the air
> with melodies abound
>
> in dense coverts on wine-dark vines
> and fruitful twigs that god has blest.
> No breezes blow, no sunlight shines,
> no storms disturb their rest.

As these melodious strains fade out, Antigone sees Creon approaching in the company of armed men (720–721):

> ANTIGONE: O land so often eulogized, the time
> has come to prove those lustrous phrases true!

Creon addresses the chorus and Oedipus in a disarming manner (729–734):

> I see a certain fear infect your eyes
> because of my abrupt arrival here,
> but there's no need for fear or ugly words.
> I haven't come with threats of force. I'm old
> and well aware I'm entering a city-state
> as powerful as any found in Greece.

He says that he's been sent by Thebes to urge Oedipus to end his miserable wandering and come back home. He should at least take pity on Antigone, who is forced to share his life of beggary.

Oedipus' response is an angry denunciation. He says that when he begged to stay in Thebes, Creon forced him out. Now that he no longer wants to be in Thebes, Creon invites him back! And yet Creon's offer is dishonest. He intends to settle Oedipus in borderlands near Thebes, where his grave won't pose any threat to the city, but he will still be an exile. Oedipus will never agree to that.

Since persuasion has failed, Creon turns to force. Oedipus will regret his attitude, Creon says: in fact, his men have already taken Ismene prisoner. Now he orders his soldiers to seize Antigone also. The soldiers obey, dragging her screaming off-stage. The chorus of elders, no match for armed men, does not interfere.

After Antigone is taken away, Creon and Oedipus continue to insult each other. Provoked by Oedipus' curse, Creon declares that he will seize Oedipus himself. Unfortunately for him, his armed guards all left with Antigone. Under these circumstances, one might think that the chorus would intervene, being fifteen old men versus one, but they merely cry out for help (884–886):

> Come quickly, you who rule the land,
> with all the forces you command!
> These men are getting out of hand!

Theseus, good ruler that he is, appears immediately, speaking in rapid-fire trochaics rather than the calmer iambics normally used (887–890):

> What's the clamor? What's the crime? From fear of what do you
> interrupt my sacrifice to him who rules the sea,
> this Colonus's protector. Tell me everything!
> Why have I come rushing here discomforting my feet?

Theseus is outraged to learn that Creon seized refugees without permission. He orders his army to chase down Creon's men and save the girls.

Creon tries to excuse himself by saying that he did not think that Athens would protect a patricide and the children of incest. Oedipus furiously protests that he is innocent of his so-called crimes because they were all unintentional. (This passage, Oedipus' ultimate defense, is scrutinized below.)

Theseus orders Creon to lead him to the kidnapped girls, if they are being held somewhere in Attica. Otherwise, he says, if they are being carried off to Thebes, the men that he has already dispatched will run them down. A choral song follows: a rousing, martial number that implies that Creon's men will be caught on the border by the Athenian cavalry. Logically, that scenario would leave Theseus and Creon out of the picture altogether, walking around Attica, but the choral song has both involved in the battle (1054–1058 and 1065–1066):

> . . . Theseus will soon display
> his military powers.
> We'll see the sisters safe today
> within this land of ours.
>
> . . . .
>
> Creon will trip despite his flight.
> The men Colonus bids
> to capture him are full of fight,
> as are the Theseids.

At the song's conclusion, Theseus returns with the girls and accepts credit for saving them. Asked by Oedipus exactly how she was saved, Antigone modestly defers to Theseus. Theseus in turn says that Antigone will tell Oedipus all about it later!

Theseus has something else on his mind. A suppliant has appeared at the altar of Poseidon and is asking to speak with Oedipus. On the basis of further description, Oedipus realizes that the suppliant must be his "detested son" Polyneices. He reluctantly agrees to listen to his plea.

When Polyneices enters, he tells Antigone that he is overcome by remorse at the sight of his father's wretched condition (1257–1261):

> here in a foreign land with you and clothes
> like these, these rags whose nauseating filth,
> as ancient as the ancient man himself,
> contaminates his flesh while breezes toss
> his unkempt hair above his eyeless head.

Polyneices then explains his situation to his father. He is an exile seeking to recover the home from which he has been unjustly excluded. The son's predicament is not unlike Oedipus' own, and he promises, if he is successful, to restore his father too. His only request is that Oedipus renounce his hatred. Oracles have indicated that he will be successful if he has his father's blessing. Otherwise he is doomed.

As with Creon, Oedipus' reply is an angry denunciation. In fact, he now holds Polyneices, not Creon, responsible for his banishment (1356–1357): "It's thanks / to you I'm cityless and wearing rags." The detail that Polyneices never ruled Thebes is swept away in the flood of Oedipus' rhetoric. (The whole passage is significant and is discussed below.) Oedipus curses Polyneices and his brother, dooming them to kill each other in the upcoming struggle. Polyneices leaves in despair. Antigone pities her brother and tries to persuade him to abandon his campaign. When it comes to holding a grudge, however, Polyneices is his father's son (1420–1426):

> ANTIGONE: . . . why indulge in anger, brother? What's
> the benefit of overthrowing Thebes?
> POLYNEICES: Retreat is shameful. I'm the older one.
> I can't endure my younger brother's taunts.

ANTIGONE: But think! His prophecies are coming true!
He said you'd die at one another's hands!
POLYNEICES: If that's his wish, we shouldn't disobey!

As Polyneices departs, repeated blasts of thunder are heard, alarming the chorus (1466–1470):

> *His lightning lights the sky once more.*
> *Will Zeus release his bolts? I fear*
> *they never do set forth in vain.*
> *A sheer catastrophe is near.*

Oedipus asks the choral leader to send for Theseus, who left to finish his sacrifice to Poseidon. The thunder is the sign of his own imminent death, and he has information that he must share with Theseus before he dies.

When the king arrives, Oedipus says that he must show Theseus the place where he will die and share other secret knowledge. Oedipus, who seems to have recovered his sight, guides Theseus and his daughters into the grove. The chorus sings the last of its four odes, praying that the gods of the underworld will treat Oedipus mercifully (1556–1563):

> *You who rule the midnight throng,*
> *lord Hades, if it isn't wrong*
> *for me to name in prayerful song*
> *Persephone and you,*
>
> *I pray you let the stranger go*
> *released from pain and cries of woe*
> *to reach the barren plain below*
> *where corpses lie concealed . . .*

As the song ends, an attendant enters with news of what transpired in the grove. He implies that he was part of a group that trailed Oedipus' party into the grove, but nothing was said of such companions previously, and no function is assigned to them. Of course, the real reason for the attendant's existence is dramaturgic: to report events to the audience.

Oedipus, he says, guided his daughters and Theseus into the grove. At a spot near the entrance to the underworld, Oedipus' daughters bathed him and wrapped him in fresh clothing. Then thunder sounded. The girls fell to the ground trembling and weeping (1610–1619):

> [Oedipus] hears their voices, sounding so distressed,
> gives them his hands and says, "My children, don't!
> Today of days your father is no more.
> All that I was has perished now, and you
> have shed the heavy task of care for me.
> I know how hard that was. A single word
> will melt away those weary hardships, though.
> No one will ever give you greater love
> than what you had from me. In future days,
> you'll have to carry on deprived of that."

After that, Oedipus and his daughters embrace and weep. When they finally fall silent, a voice booms forth, seeming to come from everywhere at once (1627–1628):

> "O you there, Oedipus, what's causing this
> delay? You've kept us waiting far too long!"

At that, Oedipus summons Theseus and has him and his daughters promise to assist each other in the future. He then tells his daughters to leave, since Theseus alone may see what will happen next.

Here the attendant slips in the fact that he was part of a group of observers. They all follow the departing girls, who are crying and moaning. Eventually, they look back in the direction of Oedipus and Theseus (1649–1666):

the man was gone, had simply disappeared!
Our ruler held his hands before his face,
shielding his eyes as though some dreadful act
he couldn't watch had just unfolded there.

. . . .

    Of Oedipus's death, no man could tell
what sort it was, excepting Theseus.
It wasn't any blazing bolt from god
or hurricane awakened on the sea
that ended Oedipus's life today.
Some god escorted him, or else the dark
abode of dead souls opened graciously.
No weeping marked his passing. No disease
had tortured him. His death was wonderful
if ever mortal's was. For those who think
my story mad, I offer no defense.

Asked where Antigone and Ismene are, the attendant replies that they are on their way. Their wailing is audible before they're seen (1697–1703):

> ANTIGONE: *So one can long for what seemed bad,*
> *past suffering, and there are charms*
> *in what was scorned, as when I had*
> *my father in my arms.*
>
> *O father, love, although you'll wear*
> *the nether dark eternally,*
> *you're not deprived, not even there,*
> *of love from her and me.*

At length, Theseus also arrives and tells the girls to be quiet, since Oedipus' painless death was not one to mourn excessively. Antigone asks him to show her exactly where her father's body lies. Theseus explains that Oedipus explicitly forbade him to show his resting place to anyone. The king will, however, help the girls return to Thebes, where they hope to prevent their brothers from killing each other. As usual, the chorus has the final word. As they and the actors make their exits, they chant in anapests (1777–1779):

> Now end these exchanges, and no longer try
> to stir lamentation. In every respect,
> these matters have ended as they were ordained.

Oedipus as Tragic Hero

Heroic Anger

> Have mercy! Other men have wicked sons
> and hasty tempers. Still, their friends' advice
> works like a magic spell to calm their souls.
> Consider your misfortunes, not today's,
> but those in which your parents were involved.
> In contemplating them, I'm sure you'll see
> that evil anger leads to evil ends.
> In fact, there's rather cogent proof of that
> in how your eyes' affliction came to be.
>
> (Antigone to Oedipus, 1192–1200)

Ancient Greek heroes—for example, Achilles, Odysseus, Ajax, Heracles, Theseus—are not models of virtue. They are great warriors whose abilities as such are inextricably bound up with a penchant for wildly excessive anger and aggression. The meaning of such depictions is not difficult to intuit: the very qualities that people encourage and revere in fierce warriors fighting for their countries add up to insanity in other contexts. The war hero is often unfit for normal life. Achilles' abuse of Hector's corpse in the *Iliad* epitomizes this insight, but it is hardly the only example. Many think of Homer's Odysseus as an ethically exemplary hero, and he is capable of containing his anger when it is advantageous to do so.[2] Nevertheless, the climax of his homecoming is a shocking bloodbath, the slaughter of Penelope's 108 young suitors. Odysseus beheads one of them, the priest Leodes, while he is begging for mercy (*Odyssey* 22.326–329). Afterward, Odysseus makes the maidservants who consorted with the suitors clean up the blood and gore and then has his son, Telemachus, execute them all (22.457–473). On his authority, a treacherous goatherd has his ears, nose, and genitals cut off and fed to dogs (22.474–477). If Athena had not intervened, Odysseus would have massacred the suitor's relatives (24.528).

Heroic anger is a major element in two of Sophocles' other tragedies. In *Ajax* the eponymous hero sets out to murder Agamemnon, Menelaus, and Odysseus because the armor of Achilles has been awarded to Odysseus. It is true that Athena drives Ajax mad so that he attacks and tortures herd animals instead, but the initial resolution to murder his comrades is his alone. In *The Trachinian Women*, Heracles storms a city, killing the men and enslaving the women and children, because its king refused to give his daughter Iole to Heracles as his mistress (*Trachinian Women* 281–285, 360). In other tales, Heracles' violent temper manifests itself in youth when he kills his music teacher, hitting him with a stool.[3] He also murders Iole's brother (*Odyssey* 21.24–30) and tries to wreck the temple of Delphi when the priestess refuses to purify him. He has to be restrained by Apollo and Zeus. Depictions of Apollo restraining Heracles were popular with Greek vase painters of the fifth century.[4]

Theseus was famous for eliminating monsters and evildoers on the road to Athens, for killing the Minotaur of Crete, and for unifying Attica.[5] In Euripides' *Hippolytus*, misplaced anger gets the better of him when his curse causes the death of his son, Hippolytus, falsely accused of raping his stepmother.[6]

In later life, Theseus abducted the underage Spartan princess Helen, later "of Troy," and tried to help his friend Pirithous seize Persephone, queen of the underworld.[7] Near the end of his life, he was driven out of Athens by the disaffected citizens and murdered while in exile on the island of Scyros by its king, who evidently feared him as a troublemaker.[8] Sophocles' depiction of a relentlessly virtuous Theseus is a departure from this tradition.

The Case of Oedipus

Sophocles' Oedipus is unusual among Greek heroes. Although killing Laius and his entourage showed physical prowess, his fame rests on the mental acuity required to answer the riddle of the Sphinx. There are indications of excessive anger and aggression in his character, but scholars differ on their significance. The dominant view is that Sophocles depicts Oedipus as essentially virtuous, if somewhat irascible. He killed his father and married his mother through the gods' contrivance. His imperfections lend depth and realism to his character but are not the so-called tragic flaws that led to his suffering. On the contrary, it was his virtuous determination to discover the murderer of Laius that caused his downfall. Without that, he could have ended his life in blissful ignorance of his own crimes.

This interpretation is given its best-known expression in "On Misunderstanding the *Oedipus Rex*," an essay by the great classicist E. R. Dodds. In Dodds's view, Oedipus is a symbol of human intelligence that cannot rest until it has solved all the riddles, "even the last riddle, to which the answer is that human happiness is built on an illusion."[9]

A Minority Opinion

Without deprecating Dodds's essay or its many adherents, I would argue that different ways of viewing Oedipus find equal support in the texts of the two plays. In my view, such ambiguity is characteristic of Sophocles' works and of great literature in general. That Sophocles' depiction of Oedipus has triggered centuries of debate over his guilt or innocence[10] is not a sign of ineptitude on that author's part. It is what the play was designed to do.

Whether or not he bears moral responsibility for his crimes, Oedipus is clearly characterized by the same kind of anger and aggression that is found in other heroes. His most memorable speeches are those in which he has lost his temper, at Tiresias and then Creon in *Oedipus Rex* and at poor Creon again and then Polyneices in *Oedipus at Colonus*. Other characters comment explicitly on his temper: Creon in *Oedipus Rex* (673–675), Creon and Antigone in *Oedipus at Colonus* (855, 1192–1193). There was surely an angry expression on the mask of the actor playing Oedipus.

There are different sources of anger. Achilles, for example, was concerned with his honor. It seems significant to me that what triggers Oedipus' wrath in its most famous explosion is hearing the truth from Tiresias (e.g., *OR* 362–368). What distinguishes his anger is that it is typically directed at truths that he does not like. I imagine two powerful forces colliding in his soul: his intelligence, which apprehends matters with great clarity, and his will, which is determined not to see that which he does not wish to see. In this, he is an Everyman. We are all involved to some extent in such a conflict. We strive to see ourselves as the paragons we wish to be despite ever-mounting evidence to the contrary. Oedipus raises this struggle to a heroic level of intensity. When accused, he whips himself into a state of self-righteous indignation based on willful ignorance and distortions rather than confronting truths about himself that he does not like. The syndrome is illustrated in *Oedipus Rex* when Oedipus convinces himself that Tiresias and Creon are plotting against him (345–349, 532–535). Dodds praises him for courageously uncovering the truth, but that interpretation soft-pedals Oedipus' quick transformation of his investigation of Laius' murder into a defense against Creon's supposed conspiracy. When he returns to the investigation of Laius' murder, he is driven forward by the hope of exonerating himself—not his concern with ending the plague (834–847). When the truth finally emerges so clearly that he cannot escape it in any other way, he deliberately blinds himself (1369–1390). How could that action epitomize the courageous search for truth? Greek philosophers viewed humble self-knowledge as a cardinal virtue,[11] but they never said that it was easy to achieve. In Oedipus' self-blinding I find a symbol of the lengths to which some will go to avoid it.

Blindness Freely Chosen

If *Oedipus at Colonus* were less of a tragedy, it might show how the poor wandering Oedipus gained self-knowledge at last, overcoming his angry resistance and humbly acknowledging the role that his ungovernable anger played in his downfall. Yet truly tragic heroes do not outgrow their faults. Oedipus' continuing struggles with the truth are on display throughout *Oedipus at Colonus*. The first instance occurs moments after Oedipus reveals his presence to the chorus. Asked who he is, he immediately appeals to their pity by identifying himself as one whose fate is not to be envied. Otherwise, he says, he would not have to rely on another person's eyes. The chorus infers that Oedipus has been blind since birth (149–152):

> *Ah! Were you born with eyes so dim?*
> *If so, your life's been long and grim,*
> *or so it would appear.*

Oedipus does not correct the impression, but anyone with even a vague memory of *Oedipus Rex* knows that he was not blind from birth. In fact, in the earlier play, when the leader of the chorus questions his wisdom, Oedipus insists that dashing out his eyes was the right thing to do under the circumstances and that he was fully responsible for the act (*OR* 1330–1333):

> *Apollo caused all this dismay,*
> *but it was I alone, not he,*
> *who struck my eyes. What good are they*
> *when there is nothing sweet to see?*

"Are You My Father?"

Later Creon's reference to Oedipus as a patricide elicits a brilliant defense from Oedipus (*OC* 992–996):

> Suppose someone assaulted you right now
> with deadly force, you righteous man, would you
> ask him, "Are you my father, sir?" or fight?
> Assuming that you're fond of life, you'd fight,
> not cast about for legal precedents.

The defense seems unanswerable until it is juxtaposed to Oedipus' own earlier description of the event from *Oedipus Rex*—before he knew that one of his victims was Laius. He is talking to Jocasta (*OR* 800–813):

> With you, I'll be completely honest. I
> had gotten near the triple path on foot.
> A herald met me there together with
> a man aboard a carriage drawn by colts,
> like you describe. The leader tried to block
> my progress using force. The older man
> did too. I hit the driver angrily
> for pushing me away. The older man
> withdrew until I crowded past, then took
> a double cattle prod and struck my head!
> He didn't pay an equal price. In brief,

> he felt the walking stick I had in hand,
> fell backward off the cart and rolled away,
> and then I slaughtered everyone.

Here the encounter seems to have been one of gradually esca-
lating violence, not the sudden ambush of Oedipus' later
memory. A cattle prod is not a deadly weapon.[12] In any event,
there actually was time for Oedipus to consider whether Laius
might be his father, especially in view of the oracle that he had
just received. The fact that a herald was present is provided by
Jocasta and is an embarrassment to Oedipus' case. It may be
significant that Oedipus changes him from a "herald" to the
group's "leader" as he tells his story. A normal herald would
have initiated the encounter by asking Oedipus to make way
for a king, and any normal solitary traveler would have com-
plied. Even if Laius' herald happened to be unusually truculent,
heralds were sacred figures. Killing one was a monstrous act in
itself.

According to Dodds, we should not judge Oedipus adversely
because none of the characters in the play do, and we must be
guided in interpretation by what is actually said. Perhaps, but
surely there are exceptions to such a rule. Sophocles must have
known that Oedipus' "then I slaughtered everyone" was going
to raise some eyebrows.

Volitional Ignorance

When confronted by Creon with his incestuous marriage to
Jocasta, Oedipus' defense is the simple assertion that neither he
nor she knew that she was his mother. Of course, he does not
mention the mental blindness that he and Jocasta displayed in
not discovering their previous relationship. Oedipus knew that
he was predicted to kill his father and had mutilated ankles and
that there was some doubt about the identity of his biological

parents. Jocasta knew that her son was predicted to kill his father and had mutilated ankles and that Oedipus had mutilated ankles. That they never put two and two together implies a lack of curiosity that could be dismissed as just a weakness in the plot. I prefer to think of it as a poignant symbol of the general truth that none are so blind as those who will not see. Such an interpretation, with its implicit notion of volitional ignorance, will strike some as anachronistic, but before rejecting it one should notice Tiresias' words when he first enters the scene and hears Oedipus demanding to know who killed Laius (*OR* 316–318):

> How dreadful wisdom is when wisdom brings
> no gain! I knew these matters well but I
> destroyed them. Otherwise, I hadn't come.

Apparently, he knew all along on some level that Oedipus had killed Laius and was Jocasta's son, but such knowledge was so disruptive and fraught with danger—so unprofitable—that he willfully "unknew" it. His words exemplify the willful ignorance that would explain the obtuseness of Oedipus and Jocasta and show that the phenomenon was on Sophocles' mind when he wrote the play.

Reframing the Past

Oedipus initially blames Creon for driving him into exile after the blinded king had regained his composure and asked to be allowed to stay in Thebes. What Oedipus does not mention is that at the end of *Oedipus Rex*, Creon says that he will refer the question of exile to the Delphic oracle and abide by its decision (*OR* 1440–1445). In the absence of contrary indications, it is fair to assume that that is what happened. Under those circumstances, Creon would have no choice other than banishment. The whole premise of the play is that Laius' murderer has to be killed or exiled to save the city: Oedipus himself issued the decree banishing the killer. Nevertheless, he represents his exile as Creon's arbitrary decision—until he directs his anger elsewhere.

When the time comes to rail at Polyneices, the story changes (OC 1354–1364):

> You evil creature! You'd the power once
> your brother exercises now in Thebes.
> That's when you drove your father out. It's thanks
> to you I'm cityless and wearing rags
> like these whose looks have made you sprinkle tears,
> now that you're in such dire straits yourself.
> Though I no longer weep, I never shall
> forget your homicidal treachery.
> You are the reason I've befriended grief.
> You banished me. Because of you I roam
> and beg my daily bread from other men.

Oedipus' accusation is not supported by any version of the story and contradicts the information given by Ismene (OC 367–376). In her account, the brothers first relinquished royal power to Creon. It was only recently, well after Oedipus went into exile, that they began to fight, resulting in Polyneices' exile. In no known version of the story is there a period in which Polyneices was the city's sole ruler. Oedipus' accusation is one more example of his rewriting the past to fuel his indignation. In this case, he is embellishing his self-portrait as a wronged father.

Oedipus' anger is overblown. The arguments by which Antigone persuaded Oedipus to listen to Polyneices in the first place (quoted above) should also have persuaded him to forgive his sons and try to reconcile them. Instead, Oedipus works himself up into such a fury that he calls curses down on his sons, making their mutual killing inevitable. Their blood too is on his hands.

When All Else Fails, Blame Fate

Oedipus' ultimate defense is that he was a victim of fate (*OC* 969–974):

> My father learned his fate from oracles:
> his children's hands would bring about his death.
> Explain your thought in blaming me for that!
> My father hadn't sown me yet, nor had
> my mother yet conceived me. I did not
> exist!

It is worth remembering that the era of *Oedipus at Colonus* was also that of the sophists. In drama as elsewhere, the Greeks took delight in the ability of good orators to make the weaker case seem stronger. By the same token, every well-reasoned speech was somewhat suspect. In view of that, I favor the use of critical thinking in evaluating Oedipus' defense. The argument is not nearly so decisive as it seems at first glance. The ability to foresee the future is attributed to the gods, but they rarely force people to do things. We mortals are not their puppets. In exceptional cases gods drive people crazy—for example, divinely sent madness caused Heracles to kill his wife and two sons and Ajax to slaughter herd animals—but normally actions, even those that are foretold, are the products of a hero's free choice when he is in full possession of his faculties. That is clearly true of Oedipus' killing of Laius. The fact that the gods have knowledge of the future is no defense.[13] If it were, no one would ever be guilty of anything.

As indicated above, my interpretation diverges from most scholarly opinion. I am reluctant to label contrary opinions mistaken. There is a good deal of ambiguity in both plays and subjectivity in the interpretative methods that readers use. Dodds's rule that interpretation should be strictly limited by judgments expressed in the text is too restrictive for a universal law. People are bound to think about implications found between the lines. It is impossible to know the extent to which such implications figured in the author's conscious intentions. One could even argue that the question is irrelevant. As Plato's Socrates says (*Apology* 22b–22c), poets are bad at explaining the meaning of what they write. One's understanding of their inspired words should not necessarily be limited by their conscious intentions.

Enter the Subconscious

A question that occurs to everyone is why—if Oedipus was so afraid of the oracle's predictions—he did not simply swear off the murder of older men and sexual intercourse with older women. Far from doing so, he killed the first old man he met and married an older woman at the first opportunity. By Dodds's rule, we are not supposed to ask about that because none of the characters in the play do, but the question is too obvious to avoid. Setting the issue aside as merely a weakness in the plot undermines the play's claim to psychological realism.

In my view, the logical explanation is that Oedipus, though deeply ashamed, was secretly drawn to the idea of killing his father and marrying his mother. In modern terms, he was in the grip of the subconscious desire that Freud attributed, rightly or wrongly, to all young men. Whether the general theory has any validity is an open question, but there is certainly reason to think that Oedipus himself had an Oedipus complex.[14]

Oedipus, Meet Dr. Freud: A Poetic Dialogue

SIGMUND FREUD: Where are you going, son, so hurriedly?
OEDIPUS: To any place that's far away from home.
SF: Your home's up there on Mount Parnassus then?

o: No. I was there consulting Delphi's god.
The city-state of Corinth, that's my home.
sf: And might I ask you what your question was?
o: I asked her who my parents really were.
sf: Why that? Just idle curiosity?
o: A rumor calling me a foundling spread.
It bothered me a lot. I'm not sure why.
sf: What was the Delphic oracle's reply?
o: She didn't deign to answer me but said
that I would be my father's murderer
and that my mother'd bear my progeny.
sf: You must have been delighted, hearing that!
o: "Delighted!" Hardly! I was terrified.
sf: And so you'll try escaping destiny?
o: That's right. That's why I flee my homeland now.
sf: That doesn't make a bit of sense, you know.
o: Why not? My parents live in Corinth. I
couldn't commit those crimes in other towns.
sf: But you're not certain *who* your parents are
or what the city is in which they live.
That's why you went to Delphi, isn't it?
o: Now that you mention it, I guess it is.
sf: And your supposed father, what's his name?
o: They call him Polybus. He's Corinth's king.
sf: Are you and Polybus on friendly terms?
o: The dear old man and I are very close.
sf: And not inclined to spill each other's blood?
o: Why no! It's almost inconceivable.
sf: As for your so-called mother . . .
o: Mérope.
sf: Can you imagine having intercourse
With her?
o: I'd rather die and so would she.
sf: And is she ripe for "bearing progeny"?
o: That season ended years and years ago.
sf: So what does that imply, my clever lad?
o: I've no idea what you're getting at.

SF: If Delphi's oracles are accurate,
then, clearly, Polybus and Mérope
don't fit your parents' profile very well.
O: I see your logic. No, you're clearly right.
They're likely not my parents after all.
I guess I've really known that all along.
SF: Why is it then you're rushing down this path?
O: You seem to have the answers. You tell me.
SF: Perhaps you're rushing forth to seize your fate.
O: What decent man would seize a fate like that?
SF: Perhaps, you entertain the secret wish
to kill the man who really fathered you.
O: How could that be? I never met the man.
SF: And yet he may have angered you somehow.
O: I'm not aware of anything he's done.
SF: Unless, of course, you count begetting you.
O: Of course, but after that there's nothing known.
SF: You know he didn't raise you as his own.
O: Well, no, he didn't keep me. Otherwise
I wouldn't be a foundling, which is what
all indications seem to say I am.
SF: How *do* you picture what occurred back then?
O: When I became a foundling? Let me think.
My father had the final say, of course.
A child he didn't want would be exposed.
SF: Left on a hill or empty field to die?
O: Yes, that's the foundling's normal history.
Unless a stranger intervenes, he dies
of cold or thirst or vicious animals.
SF: You mean that dogs might eat the foundling's flesh?
O: Or vultures. Anything is possible.
SF: And that's the way your father treated you?
O: The memory is slowly coming back.
SF: He ripped you from your mother's breast to die?
O: A mother always wants to keep the child.
SF: Her tears, your frantic cries were all in vain.
O: I dimly recollect her parting kiss.

Introduction

SF: How does that recollection make you feel?
O: Angry! Why I could almost . . .
SF: Kill him?
O: Yes!

Each reader has his or her own Oedipus, and that is as it should be. My Oedipus is guilty of his sins to the extent that individuals are responsible for actions involving willful ignorance and subconscious compulsions. He goes to his grave with his flaws intact. The gods receive him in a kindly fashion, not because he is a saint or even a reformed sinner, but because with all his flaws he has a kind of magnificence. He strove passionately within the limits of his character. The anger that undid him is not all bad. It is the quality that communities seek in heroes in times of conflict. He is revered for that reason. The fantasy is that the rage that tormented him will come back to life in the future to inspire Athenian troops.

The Afterlife of Heroes

The ancient Greeks did not embrace any one doctrine concerning the fate of the soul after death. In Plato's *Apology* (40c–e), Socrates seems resigned to the possibility that consciousness is simply obliterated by death, and that was apparently a widespread view. Aristotle, who tried to adhere to widely accepted beliefs, was content to remark that whether the dead participated in good and evil at all was a difficult question (*Nicomachean Ethics* 1.11.5). Poets like Homer created various pictures of the afterlife, but none of them gained Biblical status. One curious notion, however, did gain official recognition in Athens and elsewhere. It was thought that the spirits of heroes were attached to their physical remains and could return to life to bestow blessings and curses. Put simply, the Greeks were inclined to believe in ghosts. There were many shrines of long-dead heroes throughout the Greek world, the supposed gravesites of great individuals whose favor was sought through a wide variety of ritualistic actions.

The most famous Athenian example of posthumous activity was provided by Theseus himself, whose ghost was said to have fought on the Athenian side in the battle of Marathon.[15] A few years later, in 474 BCE, the Athenian general Cimon wrested control of the island of Scyros from pirates and discovered the grave of an oversized ancient warrior, declared to be Theseus, who died in exile on Scyros. His bones were dug up and reburied in Athens, where his tomb became a sanctuary for runaway slaves and the poor and oppressed in general (Plutarch, *Life of Theseus* 36.2). There is some irony in Sophocles' depiction of the living Theseus permitting Oedipus' burial in Athens, since he himself was to be denied that benefit until many years after his death.

The story of *Oedipus at Colonus* turns on the supposed potency of a hero's mortal remains. Oedipus asks Theseus for permission to die and be buried in Colonus. In return, his remains will protect Athens from Thebes. The strange proposition is made more so by the fact that Athens and Thebes were peaceful neighbors at the time, but Oedipus takes that into account with a prescient speech (*OC* 616–623):

> In Thebes it may be pleasant weather now
> for you, but Time's prolific womb gives birth
> to many nights and many days, wherein
> they shall discover some excuse for arms
> to scatter solemn bonds of amity.
> Then shall my frigid, buried corpse awake
> to warm itself on drafts of steaming blood,
> if Zeus is Zeus and lord Apollo true.

Needless to say, Athens and Thebes had in fact become bitter enemies by the time the play was written. Thebes was a major ally of Athens' enemy Sparta throughout the Peloponnesian War, lasting from 431 until 404, two years after Sophocles' death. In fact, an ancient scholiast asserts,[16] without naming a source, that once when the Athenians defeated the Thebans in battle, a report circulated that the Athenians had been aided by the ghost of Oedipus. The scholiast does not date this battle or describe any of its other circumstances. The account, however, fits nicely with an incident described by the historian Diodorus Siculus (13.72.3–9) and dated to 408—about when Sophocles must have started working on *Oedipus at Colonus*. During the latter part of the Peloponnesian War, the Spartan army occupied the Athenian countryside. In Diodorus' account, the Spartans once advanced in battle formation to within a half-mile of the city walls. The outnumbered Athenians kept their own foot soldiers inside the walls, but they deployed approximately a thousand cavalrymen in the space between their wall and the enemy line. There they engaged an equal number of enemy knights consisting predominantly of Thebans. After a long, fierce battle witnessed by their anxious countrymen on the walls, the Athenians prevailed, routing the Thebans with heavy casualties. It is just possible that this actual cavalry battle inspired Sophocles to bring his most famous creation back to life.

Oedipus at Colonus: Tradition or Invention?

The plots of Greek tragedies combine traditional legends with new twists invented by their authors. As I worked on translating *Oedipus at Colonus*, I became more and more intrigued by the question of whether Sophocles invented Oedipus' presence in Colonus or was repeating an ancient story. The invention, if that is what it was, would say a lot about Sophocles' boldness as a storyteller. He was a native of Colonus, and the little deme was at the time the center of political controversy, as we shall see.

Different Versions of Oedipus' Death

The story that Oedipus died at Colonus was one of several versions of his ultimate fate. According to the *Odyssey* (11.271–280), Oedipus continued to rule in Thebes even after the gods made his crimes known. The *Iliad* (23.677–680) refers in passing to Oedipus' funeral games in Thebes. (A minor character named Mekisteus is said to have participated in them.) We may infer that in the earliest versions of his legend, Oedipus died and was buried in Thebes and that his gravesite was no secret.

An alternative account, found in the scholia to *Oedipus at Colonus*, says that the Thebans would not permit Oedipus to be buried within their city's boundaries.[17] His friends tried burying him in a neighboring village, which led to a series of misfortunes for the villagers. Hence Oedipus' bones were removed and reburied at night in what was intended to be a secret location. Daylight revealed that the new grave was located inside the precinct of a temple of Demeter. Fearful locals asked an oracle whether they should expel Oedipus and were told not to disturb "the suppliant." His grave became a hero's shrine, the *Oedipodeion*. All of this took place in Boeotia, the region dominated by Thebes.

In both of these accounts, Oedipus dies in Thebes—he does not wander in exile looking for a place to die. The same is true of a third version, found in Pausanias, a geographer active in the second century CE. Oedipus dies in Thebes, and his bones are later brought to Athens. The gravesite chosen is not Colonus but the Areopagus or Hill of Ares in the middle of the city. A barren, rocky elevation just west of the Acropolis, the Areopagus was the meeting place of an ancient council that once exercised broad powers in Athens. Over time, its jurisdiction was reduced until it was limited to trials concerning a few specific crimes, most notably homicide. In myth, Orestes was tried and acquitted on the charge of matricide by the Areopagus council with the help of the goddess Athena. Pausanias recounts that story and continues (1.28.5–7; my translation):

> There is also an altar of Warlike Athena (on the Areopagus). Orestes dedicated it after he was acquitted. People call the unhewn stones on which defendants and prosecutors stand the stones of Outrage (*hubris*) and Unforgivingness respectively. Nearby there is a shrine of the goddesses that the Athenians call the August Ones (*Semnai*), but Hesiod refers to as the Furies (*Erinyes*) in the *Theogony*. Aeschylus first depicted them as having snakes instead of hair on their heads. There is nothing fearful in their images in this temple. There are also statues of Pluto, Hermes, and Earth. Those who have been acquitted by the Areopagus council offer sacrifices to them. So do both citizens and foreigners on other occasions. The tomb of Oedipus is located inside this precinct. After much research, I found that Oedipus' bones had been brought from Thebes. I cannot view Sophocles' account of the death of Oedipus as credible. According to Homer, Mekisteus came to Thebes to participate in funeral games when Oedipus died.[18]

Colonus or Areopagus: Which Came First?

Two different accounts of Oedipus' death and interment were centered in Athens: the Areopagus version and the Colonus version. One must have preceded the other, and the later version must have been made up with the earlier in mind. Even though it is preserved only in a late source, Pausanias, the Areopagus version is closer to Homer's in having Oedipus die in Thebes. The Colonus legend seems much more imaginative, as though invented to top an earlier story, but that may be because we have Sophocles' full-fledged version of the former and a meager two-sentence summary of the Areopagus version. But there is better evidence that the story of Oedipus' burial in the Areopagus came first: the fact that Sophocles' depiction of Colonus assimilates features of the Areopagus. The most striking feature is the supposed presence of a precinct of the Eumenides at Colonus. It was well known that such a precinct existed on the Areopagus, whereas it is doubtful that there was a shrine to the Eumenides in Colonus.[19] (If there was, it was not nearly as famous as the one on the Areopagus.)

Sophocles says that when Oedipus was last seen (1590–1594),

> He neared the steep descent with brazen steps
> that reach the underworld and stopped on one
> of many crossing paths beside the bowl
> once used for trading oaths by Pirithous
> and Theseus, eternal vows.

From there, he tells the girls to fetch water for bathing and libations. Then (1600–1602):

> The girls ascended Green Demeter's hill,
> which lay in view, and quickly did the things
> their father told them to.

As Frazer[20] pointed out, these details correspond to features of the landscape around the Areopagus—not, as far as is known, ones in Colonus. The steep descent, he says:

> must mean, as Prof. Jebb says, "a natural fissure or chasm, supposed to be the commencement of a passage leading down to the nether world." Such a fissure is the cave on the northern side of Areopagus down which the Furies passed after the trial of Orestes [Euripides *Electra* 1270–1272]. . . . Near the fissure in the Areopagus, at the western foot of the Acropolis, was a sanctuary of Green Demeter[21] . . . and at the foot of the Pnyx hill, probably in full view of the sanctuary of Green Demeter, there were in antiquity some natural springs and an important fountain[22] . . . from which Sophocles may have supposed that the daughters of Oedipus drew water. Further there was a place somewhere to the north of the Acropolis where Theseus

and Pirithous were said to have covenanted. All these coinci-
dences of Athenian topography with Sophocles's description
are in favour of the view that Sophocles knew the grave of
Oedipus beside the Areopagus and hinted at it in his play.[23]

It is as though Sophocles sought greater credence for his
new version of Oedipus' burial by blending details from the
inherited account. To the points made by Frazer, I would add
that the boulders on which Oedipus sits (*OC* 19, 196–197) seem
designed to bring to mind the Areopagus' stones of Outrage
and Unforgivingness.

The Evidence of The Phoenician Women

Even if we assume that the Colonus setting was a compara-
tively recent variant, it does not follow that Sophocles made it
up. In fact, it has been argued on other grounds that the Colonus version was already current in Athens when Sophocles
wrote his play. The evidence is a passage in Euripides' earlier
treatment of the Oedipus story, *The Phoenician Women*, presented in 408. In that play, Oedipus and Antigone are still in
Thebes when Polyneices and Eteocles kill each other in single
combat. Jocasta, alive at the start of the play, is driven to suicide by her sons' deaths. Creon takes charge. He prohibits the
burial of Polyneices, tells Antigone that she must marry his son
Haemon, and exiles Oedipus. The play ends with Antigone de-
claring that she will bury Polyneices herself and accompany her
father into exile. At one point she helps her father touch the
bodies of the dead: Eteocles, Polyneices, and Jocasta. Then this
(*Phoenician Women* 1702–1707; my translation):

> ANTIGONE: O Polyneices, dearest name I know!
> OEDIPUS: Apollo's oracle is being fulfilled.
> ANTIGONE: How so? Will you describe new evils now?

OEDIPUS: I'll die in Athens after wandering.
ANTIGONE: Which Attic parapet will welcome you?
OEDIPUS: Holy Colonus, horse god's domicile.

If Euripides wrote those lines in 408 or earlier, a story placing Oedipus' death in Colonus must have been known before Sophocles presented his play—but there is a complication. *The Phoenician Women* contains a number of lines that are suspected of being later, non-Euripidean interpolations, homages to different versions of the story, including this reference to *Oedipus at Colonus*. Elizabeth Wyckoff, a translator of *The Phoenician Women*, says that the original play covered

> more stages of the Oedipus legend than one would have thought a single play could hold. [Later, fourth-century] producers improved on this situation. Their additions brought in everything really memorable in the dramatic tradition of Oedipus which Euripides had left out, drawing freely on earlier plays from the *Seven against Thebes* to the *Oedipus at Colonus*. (This last, of course, Euripides had been unable to draw on, as he died before it was produced.). . . .
>
> . . . [T]he Creon-Oedipus-Antigone scene [*Phoenician Women* 1581–1709] we have is certainly not the one Euripides wrote. Note, for one thing, that Antigone is apparently planning both to go into exile, at once, with Oedipus and, in defiance of Creon, to bury Polyneices. This is impossible, but the author is simply assimilating his figure to both Sophoclean Antigones.[24]

Others argue in favor of Euripidean authorship; Donald Mastronarde, for example, observes that it is, in fact, typical of Euripides to include such prophetic references to related cults or legends at the end of his plays.[25]

The arguments on either side are inconclusive, but on balance I favor the hypothesis that the *Phoenician Women* passage is a later interpolation and Sophocles himself invented Oedipus'

death at Colonus. I am especially influenced by the considera-
tion that Sophocles was a native of Colonus. In addition, he
was involved in the turbulent political events that started with
a special assembly held in the temple of Poseidon in Colonus
(discussed below). Given his special ties to the place and to the
myth of Oedipus, to say nothing of his storytelling skills, Sophocles seems to be the likeliest originator of this account.[26]

Oedipus at Colonus and Athenian Politics

Reliable Sources

Sophocles, son of Ariston and grandson of the poet, produced
Oedipus at Colonus after the death of his grandfather, during
the archonship of Mikon [402/1], which was the fourth one
following the archonship of Callias [406/5], when most authorities say Sophocles died. That is clearly correct. Aristophanes in *The Frogs* in the archonship of Callias brings the tragic
poets back from the dead, and Phrynichus in *The Muses*,
which he presented with *The Frogs*, says:

> O blessed Sophocles, he lived a long
> and happy life. A clever man, he made
> a host of lovely tragedies and died
> with dignity. No evil marred his fate.[27]
>
> (my translation)

Once you let the mindless bliss
of youthful days slip by,
sorrow's bludgeons never miss
and troubles multiply.

Murder, envy, civil war,
strife and battles rage.

*They're a person's lot before
the final step: old age.*

*Then lonely, powerless, afraid,
one sees no friendly face.
Every kind of evil's made
old age its dwelling place.*
    (*Oedipus at Colonus* 1230–1238)

Modern scholars are justifiably cautious about making connections between the events depicted in Greek tragedies and those of real life. Much of the relevant chronology is problematic, and most of the biographical details about the authors are obvious fabrications. Reliable chronological information about the dramatists can be found, however, in the so-called *didaskaliai*: official lists of dramatic productions at musical and dramatic festivals. They specified the year (by archon's name),[28] the winning poet, and, in the case of drama, the name of the play. Some of these lists, carved in stone, survive today.[29] Aristotle made extensive collections of information from *didaskaliai*. Those works are lost, but the information that they contained spread via Hellenistic scholars into the "hypotheses" of plays. These are brief headnotes found on ancient manuscripts, typically consisting of plot summaries and information gleaned from the *didaskaliai*. From these we learn that Sophocles died during the archonship of Callias (406/405) or shortly before and that *Oedipus at Colonus* was produced posthumously. The hypothesis to *Philoctetes* indicates that it was produced in 409.[30] Sophocles was a prolific author: his ancient biography credits him with 123 plays. This means that he produced a trilogy and a satyr play every other year, on average, throughout his long career. Putting all of this together, it is reasonable to assume that he composed *Philoctetes* in 411 or 410 and set to work on *Oedipus at Colonus* after presenting *Philoctetes:* that is, between 409 and his death in 406/405.

In addition to the facts about drama and dramatists secured by the *didaskaliai*, Athenian political life of the later fifth century BCE is relatively well documented in the histories of Thucydides and Xenophon and others. These works enable us to say that the years in which *Oedipus at Colonus* was probably written were among the most tumultuous in Athenian history. Moreover, Athenians were looking to their tragedians for political guidance. This was doubly true of Sophocles, who was elected to important political offices at least three times.[31] The premise of Aristophanes' comedy *The Frogs*, which was written shortly after the deaths of Euripides and Sophocles, was that the state was in desperate need of a good tragedian. In the play Dionysus, god of the theater, travels to the underworld and comes back with Aeschylus.

Despite all this, tragedians refrained from overt comments on specific issues and individuals. Rather, the universal themes that they chose to dramatize were selected for their relevance to their own times.

The Many and the Few and the Theme of Exile

Politically, the assembly of all male citizens reigned supreme. Athens had an upper class of wealth and prestige, but the assembly's powers and its inflammatory orators meant that the elite "few" had more to fear from the "many" than vice versa. Moreover, the assembly was notoriously volatile. Yesterday's hero was today's scapegoat. Pericles' great claim to fame was that he stayed on top for decades without succumbing to the attacks of envious rivals. The price of prominence was the constant threat of exile or worse at the whim of an annoyed assembly.

It is not surprising, then, that Sophocles' last two tragedies concern great men in exile. Such tales had many parallels in Athenian reality. In fact, in the waning days of the Peloponnesian War, the fate of Athens was intertwined with that of one exiled nobleman in particular: Alcibiades, Pericles' nephew and ward.

Alcibiades and the Sicilian Disaster

Alcibiades made his first major appearance in history in 415 BCE. A charismatic young orator, he persuaded a wide-eyed Athenian assembly to attempt the conquest of Sicily, a costly and un-needed adventure. Alcibiades was chosen with two other generals to lead the invasion. The Athenians expected an easy victory there that would give them insuperable advantages in their simmering war with Sparta. Alcibiades no sooner took charge of this mission than enemies accused him of a religious outrage: participating in a mocking re-enactment of the Eleusinian mysteries, a capital offense. Instead of returning to Athens to be tried by an indignant assembly, he fled to his erstwhile enemies, the Spartans, for whom he became a military advisor. In Athens, Alcibiades was condemned to death in absentia. Deprived of his guidance, the Athenian invasion of Sicily was a spectacular failure. Ships and men were trapped in the harbor of Syracuse, the former destroyed, the latter killed, imprisoned, or enslaved.[32]

The panicky Athenians, expecting an all-out attack from Sparta, made every effort to rebuild their fleet and conduct affairs prudently. Athens' prosperity depended on its maritime empire and the tribute it received from a long list of Greek city-states in the Aegean and the Hellespont and on the coast of present-day Turkey. In the wake of the Sicilian expedition, Sparta built its own fleet in order to liberate Athens' subjects. The resulting naval warfare went on for eight years, from 412 to 404.[33]

A special board of ten elderly advisors was selected to help guide the state at a time when the need for fiscal austerity was apparent to everyone. The elected advisors included the eighty-four-year-old Sophocles.[34]

A question on everyone's mind was whether an effort should be made to recall Alcibiades. His military abilities were universally agreed on. Many felt that the charges against him had been trumped up by envious enemies. Moreover, he had fallen out of favor with the Spartans in the wake of an affair with the king's wife. He had been negotiating financial assistance for the Spartans with a wealthy Persian governor of Asia Minor. Having alienated the Spartans, he had taken up residence with the Persian governor and was willing to use his influence on Athens' behalf instead, if he should be invited back. What to do?

The Alcibiades question is put to Aeschylus by Dionysus in Aristophanes' *Frogs*. His answer (1432–1433; my translation):

> You shouldn't raise a lion in the state,
> but if you do, you'd better humor it.

Knights, Hoplites, and Sailors

Like other city-states, Athens faced the constant threat of class warfare. Athenians saw themselves as divided into three parts demographically. The smallest, wealthiest class was that of the *hippeis*, knights or horsemen: that is, those who could afford horses. They were followed by the hoplites or heavy infantry: those who could afford armor. The largest group consisted of citizens who could afford neither, but who could nevertheless vote in the assembly. Rowers in the fleet were an influential subset of this last group. The absolute numbers involved are not known. As will be seen, it was assumed that there were at least five thousand hoplites and knights.

The question that constantly exercised Athenian political thinkers was how power should be distributed among the three groups. The burdens of military adventures fell on the shoulders of the relatively wealthy. For the poor, war was a better proposition: they did not have to pay for it, and it created the opportunity for gainful employment—as rowers in the fleet. They tended to be hawks, and it was possible to blame Athens' misfortunes on their recklessness. There was a case to be made for a less democratic constitution that would place those who paid for the wars and did the fighting in charge.

The Coup of 411

In 411 a group of oligarchs succeeded in temporarily overthrowing Athenian democracy. They argued that if Athens replaced the assembly with a more responsible body, Alcibiades could be persuaded to return and exercise his influence with the Persians—Athens' only chance of surviving renewed hostilities with Sparta. They proposed replacing the current assembly of all citizens with five thousand members of the hoplite class or above. The new assembly would be managed by a council of four hundred leading citizens. During what might be called the public relations campaign in support of these measures, the democratic leader responsible for exiling Alcibiades was assassinated. That event chilled opposition to constitutional reform (Thucydides 8.65.2; Aristotle, *Constitution of Athens* 29–32). A special assembly approved the proposed measures, with the support of Sophocles and the other elderly advisors. The special assembly met outside the city walls in the temple of Poseidon in Colonus (Thucydides 8.67.2). The specific reason for the selection of that site is unknown. As the play emphasizes, however, Colonus was inhabited chiefly by horsemen. Hence the site reflected the assembly's upper-class sympathies.

Having gained power, the leaders of the Four Hundred quickly revealed an agenda that differed from their announced plans. They made no attempt to recall Alcibiades, obtain financial assistance from Persia, or name and convene the assembly of five thousand knights and hoplites. Instead, they began negotiations with Sparta, hoping to make peace on almost any terms (Thucydides 8.69–71).

Their actions quickly sparked opposition. One of the leaders of the Four Hundred was assassinated upon his return from negotiations with the Spartans (Thucydides 8.92.2). In a series of trials, other leaders were found guilty of various crimes. The prosecutors included former supporters of the Four Hundred, Sophocles among them. Two of the leaders of the Four Hundred who had led the effort to make peace with Sparta were found guilty of treason and executed. Their property was confiscated, and they were denied burial in Athens or anywhere in the empire.[35] A quotation in Aristotle's *Rhetoric* is best explained by the assumption that Sophocles himself prosecuted the original instigator of the oligarchic plot, Pisander, at this juncture (1419a25–30). This is the quotation that also establishes the likelihood that Sophocles played an active role in establishing the Four Hundred. Aristotle does not mention the occasion but says that Pisander was known to have asked Sophocles whether he was not one of the special commissioners who had supported the creation of the government of the Four Hundred, to which Sophocles replied: "Yes, I did, because there were no better choices." The specific charge against Pisander is unknown, but Sophocles' prosecution apparently prevailed, since Pisander fled Athens, took refuge in a nearby Spartan garrison, and was not heard from again.

For a brief time after the fall of the Four Hundred, Athens was governed by the Five Thousand. Both Thucydides (8.97.2–3) and Aristotle (*Constitution of Athens* 33.2) commend that government: Thucydides refers to it as the best government that Athens enjoyed in his lifetime. One of its first actions was to recall Alcibiades.

Meanwhile, on the Island of Samos . . .

While the government of the Four Hundred rose and fell in Athens, the fleet stationed on the Aegean island of Samos was also in political turmoil. A majority of the Athenian citizens attached to it were rowers, democratic in their sympathies. Among them, the attempt to establish an oligarchy backfired. They condemned the Four Hundred and established a government in exile dedicated to the restoration of democracy in Athens (Thucydides 8.73, 75–76, 81–82). Indeed, fear of the fleet was one of the factors that led to the collapse of the Four Hundred back in Athens. The exiled democrats did what the Four Hundred was supposed to do (and the Five Thousand would later do): they recalled Alcibiades and elected him general.

Some in the fleet favored sailing to Athens to restore democracy by force, but Alcibiades persuaded them to attend to naval warfare first. At stake was control of the Hellespont, where a Spartan fleet supported by the Persians was liberating cities from Athenian control. Early in 410 a Spartan fleet of sixty ships was stationed at one of these towns, Cyzicus, on the southern shore of the Propontis. Alcibiades managed to assemble a fleet of eighty-six ships at a nearby island without alerting the Spartans and then launched a surprise attack in a rainstorm. The Spartans were driven to shore; their general, Mindaros, was killed; their sailors fled; and their ships were captured by the Athenians. Shortly thereafter the Athenians captured a dispatch from the Spartans' second-in-command to his superiors back home. It read: "Ships gone. Mindaros dead. Men starving. Don't know what to do" (Xenophon, *Hellenica* 1.1.16–18, 23; Diodorus 13.49.5–51.8).

Philoctetes

At this juncture, Sophocles probably began composing his second-to-last play, *Philoctetes*, which was actually presented in 409. The play's eponymous hero is a great warrior who happens to have inherited the bow and arrows of Heracles. En route with other Greeks to fight at Troy, he is bitten by a serpent on a deserted island. The doctors cannot heal the wound, and his cries disturb the troops. Taking Odysseus' advice, the Greeks abandon Philoctetes and head for Troy. Ten years later they learn from an oracle that they cannot win the war without Philoctetes and the weapons of Heracles. Odysseus returns to the island with Achilles' young son to try to induce Philoctetes to rejoin the army. Guile and force fail, but as the play seems to be ending on a note of defeat, the ghost of Heracles appears and persuades Philoctetes to give up his anger and return to Troy to fulfill his heroic fate.

The stories of Alcibiades and Philoctetes are different in important ways. As a slippery politician, Alcibiades was more like Odysseus; as a relatively young warrior, more like Achilles' son. Nevertheless, the story of the restoration of a great warrior in exile must have brought Alcibiades to the minds of the Athenian audience. The story was a model of reconciliation and played into Athenian hopes that Alcibiades' return would bring victory at last.

Democracy Restored—For Better or Worse

In the wake of the fleet's victory, the euphoric Athenians restored full democracy, thus healing the breach between the city and the fleet. There is no record of the process by which the assembly of five thousand knights and hoplites was replaced by the old assembly of all citizens. In one way or another, the constitution of the Five Thousand praised by Thucydides and Aristotle was quickly abandoned. A decree from July 410 requires all citizens to swear to kill anyone who subverts the democracy or holds office after such subversion has been accomplished.[36]

Although it united the Athenian state, the restoration of democracy was a mixed blessing. It meant that the same crowd that voted to invade Sicily was back in charge. As an architect of the government of the Five Thousand, Sophocles must have had some misgivings. In any event, the democratic assembly wasted little time in flexing its muscle. A Spartan delegate arrived in Athens with an offer to make peace on the basis of the status quo. The offer was rejected by the assembly under the influence of the demagogue Cleophon, who assured them that total victory was just around the corner (Diodorus 13.52–53)— overlooking the fact that the Persians had adopted a policy of unlimited financial support for the Spartans. They had lost a fleet, but the Persians would buy them another (Xenophon, *Hellenica* 1.1.24–25).

Nevertheless, the good fortune of the fleet under Alcibiades' command continued—for a while. In 409 or 408[37] the Athenians regained control of cities on the mouth of the Bosporus: Chalcedon and Byzantium (Xenophon, *Hellenica* 1.3.8–9, 14–22).

For Alcibiades: A New High, Another Low

In 408 or 407 Alcibiades returned to Athens in triumph. After justifying himself to the assembly, he was elected general with authority over the other generals. He also led a procession to the temple of Demeter at Eleusis, where the mysteries that he had been accused of mocking were celebrated. The procession had been suspended in recent years because of the presence of Spartan soldiers in the countryside (Xenophon, *Hellenica* 1.4.10–20; Diodorus 13.68.1–69.3). The hopes encouraged by *Philoctetes* seemed to be coming to fruition.

One of the choral songs in *Oedipus at Colonus* has the theme that it is foolish to wish for an excessively long life. Perhaps it was written in the days that followed Alcibiades' recall, and shortly before Sophocles' death in the latter part of 406 or early in 405, when Athens' good fortune began to unravel.

In 407 or 406 Alcibiades entrusted command of the main fleet at Samos to a subordinate while he visited a squadron stationed further north. In his absence, the subordinate disobeyed his orders by skirmishing with the nearby Spartans and ended up losing fifteen ships. When the Athenian assembly heard about this, they angrily dismissed Alcibiades, appointing a board of ten generals to replace him. Alcibiades retired to an estate near the Hellespont (Xenophon, *Hellenica* 1.5.11–17; Diodorus 13.71).[38]

The Battle of Arginusae and the "Trial" of the Generals

The new supreme commander, Conon, quickly slipped up. He was overtaken by a larger Spartan fleet off the coast of Lesbos and ultimately trapped with forty ships in the harbor of Mitylene. He barely managed to get word of his predicament to the Athenians in the city. They rose to the occasion, raising a relief fleet of over a hundred ships. Men from all classes, even slaves, served as rowers. The ragtag armada engaged the Spartans near the Arginusae Islands, a tiny chain opposite Mitylene, defeated the Spartan fleet decisively, and liberated Conon's fleet. The historian Diodorus (13.98.5) describes the battle as the greatest ever fought between Greek fleets. It should have been remembered as Athens' finest hour, but clouds were gathering. As the battle ended, the weather turned bad. Although the Athenians had won, a number of their ships had been damaged and were sinking. The storm made it difficult, maybe impossible, to rescue their crews (Xenophon, *Hellenica* 1.6.15–35; Diodorus 13.97.1–100.4).

Eight generals had been in charge of the relief fleet. Six returned to Athens after the battle. They were arrested for failing to rescue the crews from the sunken ships and sentenced to death by a single vote in the assembly after a famous debate. Those executed included Pericles, son of the great statesman (Xenophon, *Hellenica* 1.7.1–35; Diodorus 13.101.1–103.2).

The execution of these generals—without the semblance of a fair trial—was among Athenian democracy's worst moments.

It cast a pall over Athenian affairs in what turned out to be the final year of Sophocles' life.

The Dream of Good Government

Herodotus (3.80–83) imagines a debate among Persian nobles on the best form of government: democracy, oligarchy, or monarchy. Darius, the future king, wins the debate for monarchy by comparing rule by the best individual man with democracies that foster corrupt practices and oligarchies that breed fierce rivalries. The argument seems sound as far as it goes but skips the critical question of how to identify the best individual man. Plato's *Republic* is, in effect, a detailed attempt to answer the question; it concludes that the best state would be governed by a properly educated philosopher-king. The *Republic* embodies the wish that emerged from the political debacles of the fifth century: the wish for a state that was governed as well as a wise and virtuous person governs his or her own life.

There is no direct connection between the story of *Oedipus at Colonus* and events in Athens between 408 and 405, but they are not unrelated. Against the backdrop of a volatile, vindictive, self-destructive assembly, Sophocles paints a picture of an Athens that never existed, a Camelot. The Athens of the play is emphatically not a democracy. An idealized King Theseus is in charge. Its citizens are typified by the knights of Colonus, proud landowners, somewhat obtuse but open to persuasion and happy to accept the guidance of their ruler. Under his direction, Athens is a protector of the weak and a refuge for the desperate. In a stark contrast with the Athenian assembly, Theseus is tolerant of human failings, even the most appalling (*OC* 560–568):

> . . . Don't fear you'll tell a tale
> so horrible that I'll abandon you.
> We've much in common. I was also raised
> away from home, a solitary man

confronting countless dangers all alone.
I never turn my back on homeless men,
withholding aid from those in desperate need.
I know that I'm a human being and don't
control the future any more than you.

Theseus is no imperialist either. Speaking for Athens, he boasts that he would never invade another's land (*OC* 924–926). Sophocles must have felt that his fantasy came closest to being realized during the brief reign of the Five Thousand, which he helped to create, at Colonus. He died about the time the six generals were executed.

How It All Ended

The following years saw the final defeat of the Athenian fleet and the surrender of the city to Sparta. In the wake of the surrender, Athens was again governed briefly by extreme oligarchs, "The Thirty," whose rule quickly devolved into a reign of terror. Exile and judicial murder became commonplace. The Thirty's excesses triggered the inevitable reaction. They were overthrown by an army of exiles, and democracy was restored again. Under a general amnesty, no one was to be prosecuted for crimes committed in the latest round of civil strife. During this period, in 401, *Oedipus at Colonus*, with its message of reconciliation, was produced by Sophocles' grandson.

History's spotlight fell on the Athenians next in 399 when they condemned Socrates to death for the practice of philosophy.

The Dream of Personal Immortality

Although Oedipus is a hero, he is also a man and is referred to on several occasions as an example of the hardships of the human condition (e.g., *OR* 1186–1196, 1524–1530; *OC* 1239–1248). Thus Sophocles' depiction of Oedipus' miraculous transition to a mysterious afterlife may be taken as a symbol of Everyman's ultimate fate. In classical times, belief in a desirable afterlife was institutionalized in the mysteries of Eleusis, the famous yearly rites of Demeter, Persephone, and Hades. In the myth behind the rites, Zeus's daughter Persephone is carried off to the underworld by Hades to be his bride but is rescued by Hermes and restored to her grieving mother, Demeter. Subsequently, she dwells above the ground with her mother during the spring and summer and under the earth with Hades in the winter. The rites probably included a re-enactment of Persephone's abduction and rescue. Other parts were so secret that it was a capital crime to divulge them to non-initiates—hence the gravity of the charge that Alcibiades had re-enacted them privately for his own amusement. To this day, Eleusis has kept its secret, but it is known from ancient testimonials that initiates felt assured of a happy afterlife.[39] One of the testimonials is a fragment from one of Sophocles' own lost plays (Fragment 837; my translation).

> Thrice blessed
> are mortal men who enter Hades' realm
> having beheld those mystic rites. They get
> to live, while others have all evils there.[40]

An indication that Eleusis with its promise of immortality was on Sophocles' mind is the way he weaves a reference to the rites into the chorus's description of the rescue of Antigone and Ismene. The Eumolpidae to whom he refers are an ancient Athenian clan whose members served as hierophants or high priests conducting the rites.

The chorus anticipates that the battle will occur near a certain temple to Apollo or in Eleusis, on the shores of a landlocked bay some fourteen miles northwest of Athens (1049–1058):

> *. . . on the gleaming torchlit strand*
> *where goddesses reveal*
> *their sacred rites to mortal man*
> *and place a golden seal*
>
> *on tongues of priests with whom they share*
> *their rites, Eumolpidae,*
> *their holy ministers. It's there*
> *or somewhere else nearby*
>
> *that Theseus will soon display*
> *his military powers.*
> *We'll see the sisters safe today*
> *within this land of ours.*

There is some similarity between Persephone's story and the play's action at this juncture: Theseus is like Hermes, rescuing the maidens and restoring them to their parent. Even if that similarity is just coincidental, the extended reference to the Eleusinian rites shows that they and their promise of immortality had some relevance to the story that Sophocles meant to tell.

Some of the implications of the gods' reception of Oedipus are tangled up with the question of his personal guilt or innocence. If he is viewed as an innocent victim of fate, his story is rather like Job's: the gods for their own reasons visit misery and suffering on him, but they make it all good in the end. In the view that I would favor, Oedipus is flawed and sinful to the end, but the gods in their mercy are kind to him. He has suffered enough.

A Note on Sophocles' Family Life

Many authorities say that the elderly Sophocles once defended himself against an accusation of dementia by reciting the parodos from *Oedipus at Colonus*,[41] which begins:

Horse country here, Colonus, where
the finest farms on earth are found,
and nightingales who fill the air
with melodies abound . . .

The song seemed so wonderful that Sophocles departed
from the courtroom amid cheering and applause, as if he were
leaving the theater.

(Plutarch, "Whether an Old Man Should Engage in Politics,"
Moralia 785A–B, my translation)

Like so many colorful anecdotes about ancient authors, this is
in all likelihood an apocryphal tale inspired by events in
Sophocles' fictional works—notably, the hostility between
Oedipus and his sons, Polyneices and Eteocles.[42] Sophocles
had two sons, Iophon and Ariston, and a grandson, Sophocles.
Iophon and the younger Sophocles were also playwrights and
enjoyed some success: in fact, Aristophanes (*Frogs* 69–72) refers
to Iophon as Athens' best surviving dramatist following the
deaths of his father and Euripides. The young Sophocles is best
remembered for having produced *Oedipus at Colonus* in 401, a
fine tribute to his grandfather's memory. The fact that son and
grandson followed in his footsteps, together with Sophocles'
reputation for affability, suggests that he and his progeny got
along better than Oedipus and Polyneices.

Notes

1. Creon's plan is reminiscent of an alternative account of Oedipus'
burial found in the scholia to *Oedipus at Colonus* 91. See V. de Marco, *Scholia
in Sophoclis Oedipeum Coloneum* (Rome: Bretschneider, 1952), 11; also *Fragmente der griechischen Historiker* 382.2. According to this, Oedipus' friends
were barred from burying him in Thebes proper but eventually laid him to
rest on its outskirts in the tiny Boeotian town of Eteonus.

2. E.g., *Odyssey* 20.10–21, where Odysseus manages to contain himself
when he hears his maidservants sneaking off to meet with their lovers.

3. The only classical sources for this story are vase paintings. The earliest literary sources are Diodorus and Apollodorus. See T. Gantz, *Early Greek Myth: A Guide to Literary and Artistic Sources* (Baltimore: Johns Hopkins University Press, 1993), 379.

4. See Gantz, *Early Greek Myth*, 437–38.

5. See Gantz, *Early Greek Myth*, 249–55 and 262–70. Thucydides (2.15.2) credits Theseus with the unification of Attica.

6. Euripides' *Hippolytus* emphasizes the remorse that Theseus feels when he realizes that his dying son is innocent. Theseus thus resembles Oedipus in causing the death of his son by means of a curse. Like Oedipus too he is responsible for his father's death. The well-known story is that Theseus forgot to change black sails to white as a signal of success on the ship that was bringing him back from Crete. Seeing the black sails, his father killed himself; see Gantz, *Early Greek Myth*, 276.

7. See Gantz, *Early Greek Myth*, 288–95.

8. See Gantz, *Early Greek Myth*, 297–98.

9. E. R. Dodds, "On Misunderstanding the *Oedipus Rex*," *Greece and Rome* 13 (1966): 48.

10. See Michael Lurje, *Die Suche nach der Schuld: Sophokles' Oedipus Rex, Aristoteles' Poetik und das Tragödienverständnis der Neuzeit* (Munich: K. G. Sauer, 2004), a survey of the controversy from the Renaissance forward.

11. The thought behind the motto "Know thyself!" was the critical importance of recognizing one's own limitations. For an exposition of this idea, see especially Plato's *Philebus* 48c–49a and Xenophon's *Memorabilia* 4.2.25.

12. The Greek word is *kentron*, used elsewhere to denote bee stings. We should probably picture a flexible switch with a metal barb. It would have been designed to irritate, not to kill or even to wound seriously.

13. Dodds, "On Misunderstanding the *Oedipus Rex*," 42–43, cites B. Knox, *Oedipus at Thebes* (New Haven: Yale University Press, 1957), 39, who makes this point with the example of Jesus prophesying that Peter would deny him three times. Jesus' foreknowledge did not exonerate Peter.

14. Oddly, Freud did not think that Oedipus exemplified the complex; rather, he was an innocent victim of fate. In Freud's view, the audience's fascination with Oedipus' story was evidence of their own subconscious Oedipal desires, but Oedipus himself was in the clear.

15. The ghost of Theseus was depicted emerging from the earth during the battle in a painting in the *Stoa Poikile*, a colonnade housing art works on

the edge of the agora. The Marathon painting is described by Pausanias (1.15.3). Herodotus (1.66–68) tells a similar story about the Spartans, who were unable to defeat the neighboring Tegeans until they recovered the bones of Orestes.

16. Scholia on Aelius Aristides, *To Plato: In Defense of the Four,* 172, cited by Lowell Edmunds, *Theatrical Space and Historical Place in Sophocles' Oedipus at Colonus* (Lanham, MD: Rowman and Littlefield, 1996), 96; printed in W. Dindorf, *Aristides,* 3 vols. (Hildesheim: Georg Olms, 1829/1964), 3:560. Aristides likens Hesiod's statement that the members of the age of gold became friendly spirits under the earth (*Works and Days* 122–26) to "Oedipus lying in Colonus." The scholiast comments: "It's said that after his misfortunes, Oedipus came to Athens. Feeling pity, the gods granted him glory as a protector of Attica. Others say that he was the cause of many evils to the Thebans. Being cursed on account of the deaths of his sons, he was banished from the city, came to Colonus, and was buried there when he died. Once when the Thebans were marching against the Athenians, Oedipus appeared to the Athenians and ordered them to prepare to do battle courageously against the Thebans. The Athenians charged and routed the Thebans" (my translation).

17. V. de Marco, *Scholia,* 91.

18. Valerius Maximus, a writer of the first century CE, describes (5.3.3) the grave of Oedipus, venerated by the Athenians, as lying between the Areopagus and the Acropolis.

19. The only evidence for the existence of such a sanctuary on Colonus is a terracotta roof tile that was reused as the cover of a second-century BCE grave located a half-mile from Colonus. Excavated in 1988, the tile bore the stamped inscription *semnôn theôn* ("of the august goddesses"). The excavator suggested that the tile came from their shrine on Colonus, which may have been destroyed by the Macedonian troops that laid siege to Athens during the so-called Chremonidean War (c. 267–261 BCE). See *Supplementum Epigraphicum Graecum* 38 (1988), 265.

20. J. G. Frazer, *Pausanias's Description of Greece*, translated with a commentary (New York: Biblo and Tannen, 1965), 2:366–67.

21. The sanctuary of Green Demeter is mentioned by Aristophanes (*Lysistrata* 831). The women who have seized the Acropolis see a man hurrying up the slope past it.

22. The so-called Southwest Fountain House lay on the southwestern edge of the agora in full view of the Areopagus. See Frazer, *Pausanias's Description of Greece*, 2:112–18; J. Camp, *The Athenian Agora: Excavations in the Heart of Classical Athens* (London: Thames and Hudson, 1986), 156–57.

23. Pausanias (1.18.4) notes the location somewhere around the Acropolis of "the place where people say that Pirithous and Theseus made their pact when setting out to Lacedaemon and later to the Thresprotians" (my translation). The reference is to their abduction of Helen and the attempt to seize Persephone. Plutarch (*Theseus* 27.7) may refer to the same place as the *Horkōmosion* ("the oath-taking place"), which was near the temple of Hephaestus on the northwestern edge of the agora.

24. E. Wyckoff, "Introduction to *The Phoenician Women*," in *Euripides V* (Chicago: University of Chicago Press, 1959), 68–69.

25. Euripides, *Phoenissae*, edited with introduction and commentary by D. J. Mastronarde (Cambridge: Cambridge University Press, 1994), 626 (on lines 1703–7).

26. One more passage cited as evidence of a pre-Sophoclean tradition that Oedipus was buried in Athens comes from a Homeric scholiast quoting Androtion, a fourth-century BCE politician and—after being exiled—historian: "Banished by Creon, Oedipus came to Attica and settled in the deme of the horseman Colonus. He was a suppliant in the precinct of the Goddesses Demeter and Athena the Protector. Assaulted by Creon, he obtained (the protection of) the warrior Theseus. Dying of old age, Oedipus urged Theseus not to show his grave to any Theban, since he did not want them to mutilate his corpse" (*Fragmente der griechischen Historiker* 324.62). Edmunds (*Theatrical Space*, 96) argues that Androtion's source is probably not Sophocles, since his account differs in some detail from the playwright's. To me, Androtion's account sounds like a rationalized version of Sophocles' plot. It is especially telling that Oedipus dies of old age.

27. The second of four "arguments" transmitted with the text of *Oedipus at Colonus* in de Marco, *Scholia*, 2, and R. C. Jebb, *Sophocles: Plays, Oedipus Coloneus* (London: Bristol Classical Press, 2004), 4. Compare Phrynichus fr. 31 in Kock, *Comicorum Atticorum Fragmenta* 1.379.

28. The chief archon, selected annually by lot, was Athens' highest-ranking civilian official, responsible for organizing certain religious festivals and trials concerning family matters. The archon entered office in midsummer.

In our terms, he served roughly from one July to the next. Hence "the year of Callias," for example, is usually translated as 406/405 BCE, and stands approximately for the span of time from July 406 through June 405. The references to July and June are also approximations, since the Greeks used a lunar calendar.

29. See *Inscriptiones Graecae* 2² 2318, 2319–23.

30. During the archonship of Glaukippos, 410/409 BCE. Since the Dionysian festival in which the play was presented was held in early spring, the date is roughly equivalent to March 1, 409. See note 28 above.

31. The Athenian Tribute Lists name "Sophocles of Colonus" *Hellenotamias* (treasurer of the Delian League) for the year 443/442; see B. Meritt et al., *Athenian Tribute Lists II* (Cambridge, MA: Harvard University Press, 1949), 18. The Aristides scholia (Dindorf, *Aristides*, 3:485) quote Androtion (*Fragmente der griechischen Historiker* 324.38) as naming "Sophocles from Colonus, the poet" as one of ten generals (including Pericles) in charge of the war against the rebellious ally Samos in 441/440. Cf. S. Radt, *Tragicorum Graecorum Fragmenta IV: Sophocles* (Göttingen: Vandenhoeck and Ruprecht, 1977), 44. For Sophocles' service as a special advisor in 412/411, see note 34 below. For a survey of all the evidence for Sophocles' political activities, see Robin Osborne, "Sophocles and Contemporary Politics," in *A Companion to Sophocles*, ed. Kirk Ormand (Chichester, West Sussex: Wiley-Blackwell, 2012), 270–86.

32. Thucydides' Books 6 and 7 are the primary source for the Sicilian expedition and Alcibiades' role in it.

33. Thucydides' Book 8 is the primary source for the eventful first year of the naval war. The story is picked up by Xenophon's *Hellenica*.

34. Thucydides (8.1.3) mentions the appointment of a committee of elders in 413; Aristotle's *Constitution of Athens* (29.2) adds that the committee had ten members originally, was expanded to thirty in 411, and was charged with proposing whatever measures were deemed necessary for the salvation of the state. (In Thucydides 8.67.1 a newly elected committee of ten is given that charge.) The evidence for the remarkable fact that Sophocles was a member of the commission is a quotation in Aristotle's *Rhetoric* (1419a25–30) in which he admits that he was one of the commissioners who voted to establish the government of the Four Hundred. He says that it was a wicked thing to do but that there were no better alternatives. For a compelling case that Aristotle's

Sophocles was the tragedian, not a different Sophocles, see Michael H. Jameson, "Sophocles and the Four Hundred," *Historia* 20 (1971): 542–46.

35. See Jameson, "Sophocles and the Four Hundred," 551, for the text of the chilling condemnation; it is also found in *Fragmente der griechischen Historiker* 342.5b.

36. Andocides 1.96–98. On the date of the decree, see Georges Dalmeyda, ed., *Andocide Discours* (Paris: L'Association Guillaume Bude, 1966), 47, n. 1.

37. The exact dates of several events from this period are disputed because Xenophon's year-by-year account omits a year. The dates I give are taken from David Thomas, "Chronological Problems in the Continuation," in *The Landmark Xenophon's Hellenika*, ed. Robert Strassler (New York: Pantheon Books, 2009), 331–39.

38. Diodorus (13.73.3–74.4) adds that Alcibiades was accused of numerous other misdeeds and went into voluntary exile in the belief that Athens was no longer safe for him.

39. See George Mylonas, *Eleusis and the Eleusinian Mysteries* (Princeton: Princeton University Press, 1961), 282: "[the rites] gave the initiate confidence to face death and a promise of bliss in the dark domain of Hades whose rulers became his protectors and friends through initiation."

40. Quoted by Plutarch ("How to Study Poetry," 21f). Plutarch reports that Diogenes objected to these lines because of the implication that horrible sinners could be saved by participating in the rites, whereas real heroes, like Epaminondas, would suffer merely for not participating. Of course, lines spoken by one of his characters do not necessarily embody Sophocles' beliefs.

41. Plutarch's mistake. The passage cited is from the first choral song or "stasimon" after the parodos.

42. The ultimate source of the story is the anonymous life of Sophocles transmitted in the ancient manuscripts of his plays: "It is said in many sources that (Sophocles) was once sued by his son Iophon. Iophon was his son by Nicostrate; Ariston, his son by Theoris of Sicyon. Sophocles preferred Ariston's son, who was also named Sophocles, to Iophon. Once in a drama, he (?) represented Iophon as being jealous and accusing his father of senility before their clansmen. Their clansmen, however, fined Iophon. Satyrus quotes Sophocles as saying, 'If I am Sophocles, I am not crazy. If I am crazy, I am not Sophocles.' Then he read *Oedipus*" (Radt, *Fragmenta IV*, 34–36; my translation). As is well known from Aristophanes' *Clouds*, comic dramatists

often caricatured prominent Athenians, and these caricatures are a frequent source of apocryphal biographical anecdotes by Hellenistic writers like Satyrus. A comedy of this kind is probably the source that Satyrus quotes. As it stands, the text implies that Sophocles himself dramatized this scene, but that is unlikely in the extreme. Probably, as Jebb suggests, the name of some comic poet has been omitted by mistake (*Sophocles: Plays, Oedipus Coloneus*, xli). The inspiration for the story was probably not real life, but characters and events from *Oedipus at Colonus*, with Sophocles likened to Oedipus, Iophon to the jealous older brother Polyneices, and Sophocles junior to Eteocles. Though apocryphal, the story is evidence of the high regard in which the elderly Sophocles was held by his fellow Athenians.

Introduction

Pronunciation Guide and Glossary of Proper Names

Key

ə: as in the first and last syllable of *America*
a: as in *bat*
ä: as in *father*
ā: as in *say*
e: as in *get*
ē: as in *be*
i: as in *it*
ī: as in *eye*
ō: as in *go*
ü: as in *loose*

Adrastus (ə-dras´-təs): king of Argos, Polyneices' father-in-law.
Aegeus (ē´-jē-əs): king of Athens, Theseus' father.
Aetolia (ē-tō´-lē-ə): region in west central Greece.
Amphiaraus (äm-fē-ə-rā´-əs): Argive prophet, slain in the expedition against Thebes.
Antigone (an-tig´-ə-nē): Oedipus' daughter.
Aphrodite (a-frō-dī´-tē): goddess of love.
Apia (a´-pē-ə): alternative name for the Peloponnesus.
Apollo (ə-pä´-lō): god of prophecy, worshiped at Delphi.

Arcady (är´-kə-dē): the central Peloponnesus.

Areopagus (er-ē-ä´-pə-gəs): "hill of Ares," a hill in Athens next to the Acropolis, meeting place of an ancient judicial council.

Ares (er´-ēz): god of war.

Argos (är´-gōs): city and region of southeastern Peloponnesus.

Atalanta (a´-tə-lan´-tə): legendary heroine renowned for running and resistance to marriage.

Athena (ə-thē´-nə): wise warrior goddess of Athens.

Bacchanalian (ba-kə-nā´-lē-ən): associated with Bacchus or Dionysus.

Cadmeia (kad-mē´-ə): city of Cadmus, a name for Thebes.

Capaneus (ka´-pə-nüs): boastful warrior slain in the expedition of the seven against Thebes.

Cephisus (se´-fə-səs): river in Attica flowing past Colonus on the west.

Colonus (kə-lō´-nəs): Attic deme or township, a mile and a half north of the Acropolis.

Creon (krē´-ən): Oedipus' brother-in-law, new king of Thebes.

Delphi (del´-fī): the site of Apollo's oracular temple.

Demeter (di-mē´-ter): goddess of agricultural abundance, also associated with the underworld.

Dionysus (dī-ə-nī´-səs): also known as Bacchus, god of wine and revelry.

Erinyes (ir-re´-nē-ēz): Greek term for the Furies, known euphemistically as the Eumenides ("Kindly Ones") and the Semnai ("Holy Ones").

Eteocles (ē-tē´-ə-klēz): Polyneices' younger brother.

Eteoclus (ē-tē´-ə-kləs): warrior slain in the expedition of the seven against Thebes.

Eumenides (yü-men´-ə-dēz): Kindly Ones, euphemism for the Erinyes (Furies).

Eumolpidae (yü-mōl´-pə-dī): priestly family who supervised the rites of Hades, Demeter, and Persephone at Eleusis.

Hades (hā´-dēz): god of the underworld.

Helios (hē´-lē-əs): god of the sun.

Hermes (hər´-mēz): messenger god, guide of dead souls to the underworld.

Hippomedon (hə-pä´-mə-dän): warrior slain in the expedition of the seven against Thebes.

Ismene (is-mā´-nē): Antigone's sister.

Labdacid (lab-dä´-kid): descendant of Labdacus, an early king of Thebes.

Laius (lī´-əs): Oedipus' father.

Nereids (nir´-ē-ids): sea goddesses, daughters of Nereus, an old merman.

Oea (ē´-ə): deme west of Colonus.

Oedipus (e´-də-pəs): king of Thebes who killed his father and married his mother.

Oeneid (ē´-nē-id): descendant of Oeneus, i.e., Tydeus, a great warrior slain in the expedition of the seven against Thebes.

Olympus (ō-lim´-pəs): mountain home of the gods in northern Greece.

Pallas (pa´-ləs): alternative name for Athena.

Parthenopaeus (pär-then´-ə-pē´-əs): son of Atalanta, slain in the expedition of the seven against Thebes.

Pelops (pē´-läps): ancient hero from whom the Peloponnesus took its name.

Persephone (pər-se´-fə-nē): goddess of the underworld, married to Hades.

Phoebus (fē´-bəs): another name for Apollo.

Pirithous (pir´-i-thüs): Theseus' comrade.

Polyneices (pä-lə-nī´-sēz): son of Oedipus.

Poseidon (pə-sī´-dən): god of horses and of the sea.

Poseidonion (pō-sī-dō´-nē-ən): temple of Poseidon.

Prometheus (prō-mē´-thē-əs): Titan renowned for giving mankind fire.

Pytho (pī´-thō): another name for Delphi.

Rhea (rē´-ə): Titan, mother of the elder Olympian gods (Zeus, Hera, Poseidon, Demeter) and Hades.

Stygian (sti´-jē-ən): associated with the Styx, a river in the underworld.

Talaus (tə-lā´-əs): Hippomedon's father.

Tartarus (tär´-tə-rəs): abyss of the underworld.

Thebes (thēbs): city in Greece once ruled by Oedipus.

Theseids (thē´-sē-ids): children of Theseus, applied metaphorically to all Athenians.

Theseus (thē´-sē-əs): king of Athens, slayer of the Minotaur.

Thoricus (thōr´-ə-kəs): a hill in Attica.

Tydeus (ti´-dē-əs): hero slain in the expedition of the seven against Thebes.

Zeus (züs): king of the gods.

Oedipus at Colonus

Characters

OEDIPUS, exiled king of Thebes
ANTIGONE and ISMENE, Oedipus' daughters
THESEUS, king of Athens
CREON, Oedipus' brother-in-law
POLYNEICES, Oedipus' elder son
STRANGER, a resident of Colonus
ATTENDANT, a soldier attending Theseus (others attending
  · him and Creon are mute)
CHORUS and CHORAL LEADER, elders of Colonus

(The play is set in Colonus, a suburb of Athens, a little
more than a mile north of the city walls. The backdrop
is a thicket of trees and vines. There is an opening in the
middle where a path leads into the thicket's interior.
Two boulders lie on the stage, one closer to the thicket,
the other closer to the orchestra, where the chorus performed. Elsewhere on the stage is an equestrian statue
representing Colonus, the legendary founder of the
settlement. There are entrances on either side of the
stage, one leading southeast to Athens, the other northwest to Thebes. OEDIPUS and ANTIGONE enter from
the Theban side. ANTIGONE leads OEDIPUS, who

keeps a hand on her shoulder for guidance. They stop
by the boulder near the thicket.)

OEDIPUS:
Old blind man's loving child, Antigone,
what region's this we've entered? Whose domain?
Who shall receive the homeless Oedipus
today, extending meager charity?
I ask for little, getting even less,
but less than little's adequate for me.
Time, suffering, my noble nature third
have taught me how to cherish what I have.
  But, child, if you can see a resting place,
an open field or sacred grove, let's stop   10
and learn our whereabouts.[1] We're strangers here.
We need to ask the local citizens
for help, and do whatever they advise.

ANTIGONE:
Poor father, Oedipus, to judge by sight
the city walls are rather far away.
This spot is clearly sacred, though. It's full
of olives, laurel trees, and vines with crowds
of sweetly singing nightingales within.
So rest your limbs on this unpolished stone.
You've traveled far, considering your age.   20

OEDIPUS:
Come help me sit while keeping watch. I'm blind.

---

1. The answer, Colonus, was a politically charged name for Sophocles'
audience and is delayed until line 59 for dramatic effect. See introduction,
page lii.

ANTIGONE (lowering OEDIPUS onto the boulder):
There isn't any need to tell me that.

OEDIPUS:
Have you got any notion where we are?

ANTIGONE:
We're close to Athens. Otherwise, I'm lost.

OEDIPUS:
We've heard as much from every traveler.

ANTIGONE:
Should I go ask somebody where we are?

(Enter Athenian STRANGER with a concerned look.)

OEDIPUS:
Yes, child—if there are people hereabouts.

ANTIGONE:
There are. In fact, I needn't look for them,
for I can see another person now.

OEDIPUS:
What's that? How so? Is someone drawing near?   30

ANTIGONE:
No, not precisely. He's already here.
So say whatever suits the moment best.

OEDIPUS (rising to speak):
Hearing from her whose eyesight serves both her

and me that you'd arrived, the perfect man
to help us scatter clouds of ignorance . . .

STRANGER:
Say nothing more until you leave that place.
It's sacrosanct. Trespassing's not allowed.

OEDIPUS:
But what's it called? Which god is worshiped here?

STRANGER:
It's holy ground where no one dwells. Dread gods,
daughters of Earth and Darkness, claim the spot.   40

OEDIPUS:
What sacred name should I employ in prayer?

STRANGER:
The people here call them Eumenides,
all-seeing ones, but other names are used.[2]

OEDIPUS:
I pray they kindly take a suppliant.
I never mean to leave this resting place.

2. Eumenides, "Kindly Ones," was a euphemism used in Athens for the
Erinyes, "Furies," underworld goddesses who punished heinous sins such as
patricide and incest. They were also known as the *Semnai*, "August Ones."
They are depicted in action in Aeschylus' *Eumenides*. Pausanias (1.28.6)
mentions a sanctuary of the Eumenides near the Areopagus on the edge of
the Athena agora. There is no record of one in Colonus. See introduction,
page xliv.

STRANGER:
Why not?

OEDIPUS:
        My fortune's covenant decrees.[3]

STRANGER:
Well then, I won't presume to banish you
without the city sanctioning the act.

OEDIPUS:
But don't forget my questions, even though
I'm just a homeless man, as you can see.   50

STRANGER:
Say what they are. I'll honor your request.

OEDIPUS:
This neighborhood we've entered—what's it called?

STRANGER:
I'll tell you all I know, so listen well.
It's dread Poseidon's realm, a sacred place.[4]
The fire-bringing god Prometheus,

3. When, as happens here, a single verse is divided between characters, I
indicate the rapid change of speaker by indenting the second (and sometimes
the third) line. Such complementary metrical units are treated as a single
item for line-counting purposes.

4. Thucydides (8.67.2) confirms the existence of a temple of Poseidon in
the deme of Colonus. Its precinct was used in 411 BCE for the assembly that
replaced the democracy with a short-lived oligarchy. See introduction, page
lii.

the Titan, also dwells within,[5] but where
you're standing—that's the Brazen Avenue,
the prop that anchors Athens.[6] Fields nearby
say this equestrian

(Pointing to the statue.)

Colonus first
united them. They're all together now,   60
a single entity that bears his name.
Such is the neighborhood surrounding you,
famed less in poetry than daily life.

OEDIPUS:
In other words, it *is* inhabited?

5. Possibly a reference to an altar dedicated to Prometheus, mentioned
by Pausanias (1.30.2) as a feature of Plato's Academy, which was next to
Colonus.

6. "Brazen" here is probably used in a figurative sense to mean rocky.
The phrase is nicely explained by Valdis Leinieks in The *Plays of Sophokles*
(Amsterdam: B. R. Grüner, 1982), 180–82: the heart of Colonus was a limestone hill seated on the southern edge of a limestone platform and facing a
second hill a quarter-mile to the north. A road passing over the limestone
platform between the two hills was called the *chalkopous hodos*, literally the
"bronze-footed passage," because the ground was hard and flanked by hills
on either side. The road continued north around Mount Aegaleos and thence
to Thebes. Heading south, it led toward Athens. For the purpose of the play,
at least, it terminated in the "steep descent with brazen steps / that reach the
underworld" (1590–1591). Why Sophocles calls the Brazen Avenue "the prop
that anchors Athens" is unclear. Perhaps it represents Athens' connection
with the gods of the underworld and their sobering influence.

STRANGER:
Yes, and the people take their name from him.

(He points to the statue again.)

OEDIPUS:
Who rules? Or do the people have the say?

STRANGER:
The city's king is also sovereign here.[7]

OEDIPUS:
Who's that? Whose strength and reason reign supreme?

STRANGER:
That's Theseus, old Aegeus's son.

OEDIPUS:
Would you consider sending word to him?   70

STRANGER:
Concerning what? Some favor sought by you?

OEDIPUS:
A little one he'll profit greatly from.

STRANGER:
What profit could a sightless man confer?

OEDIPUS:
All of my words will have unerring sight.

7. As discussed in the introduction (page lviii), Theseus' Athens is emphatically not a democracy.

STRANGER:
My friend, for I don't wish you any harm,
if you're as noble as—apart from fate—
you seem to be, don't venture off that spot
until I tell the local residents;
for they and not the city folk will say
if you may stay or have to travel on.[8]   80

(Exit STRANGER toward Athens.)

OEDIPUS:
What's happened? Is the stranger gone, my child?

ANTIGONE:
He is, so you may speak more freely now,
my father. I'm your only company.

OEDIPUS (praying):
O goddesses of fearsome countenance,
since I've approached your sanctuary first,
treat me and lord Apollo graciously.
When he foretold my many sufferings,
he said I'd find this resting place in time,
and it would mark my journey's end. He said
that I'd be welcomed where great goddesses   90
reside, and there I'd end my sorry life.
He added that I'd benefit my hosts,
but be the bane of those who banished me.
He promised there'd be signs of those events:

8. This statement contradicts lines 47–48, in which the stranger says
that he must consult the city. Perhaps he is being characterized as somewhat
befuddled. There is no obvious explanation for his waffling. His decision to
involve the local citizens explains the appearance of the chorus at line 117.

the earth would shake and Zeus's thunder roar.
It must have been an omen sent by you
and not some random bird that guided me
to this, your wooded grove. For otherwise
how could my travels bring me straight to you,
a sober man to wineless goddesses,[9]   100
or find this holy seat of natural stone?
    Come, goddesses, fulfill Apollo's words
and grant me closure. Let me pass away—
unless I seem too lowly, having been
enslaved to mankind's cruelest suffering.
    Sweet children, born of ancient Darkness, come!
Athens, the city most renowned of all,
the child of Pallas, greatest goddess, come!
Pity this wretched phantom Oedipus,
for what you see is not my former self.   110

ANTIGONE:
Quiet! Some people come this way. They're old—
your resting place's guardians, no doubt.

OEDIPUS:
Yes, I'll be quiet. Meanwhile, help me off
the path. I'll hide inside this thicket now
in hopes of learning what they have to say.
It's learning that's the key to prudent acts.

      (Led by ANTIGONE, OEDIPUS steps inside the
      thicket.)

    9. Libations of wine were never offered to the grim Erinyes. As a
wandering beggar, Oedipus also goes without wine and other luxuries.

CHORUS (entering hurriedly from the
Athenian side):   Parodos[10] (117–253)
Who was the man and where's he now?[11]   Strophe A[12] (117–137)
He's disappeared. We wonder how.
The boldest man of all!

He's surely wandered far and wide.
No native son would step inside
the grove of savage maids,

the maids unnamed among the wise.
We pass them by with shaded eyes,
our lips form silent prayers.

Our thoughts are pious, mouths are dumb.
And now we've heard that someone's come
who disrespects the maids.

I'm scanning all the sacred ground
in search of him, but haven't found
the place where he's concealed.

10. *Parodos* ("side entrance") is the term applied by Aristotle to the song
sung by a tragic chorus as it first enters the dancing area at the foot of the
stage. I have not attempted a line-by-line translation of choral songs or other
lyric passages. For each section of such passages I provide the corresponding
line numbers from the Greek text. Thus the parodos' first stanza or "strophe"
(117–137) corresponds in meaning to twenty-one lines in the Greek text even
though it takes up only fifteen lines in my translation. In spoken passages, there
is an exact correspondence between my line numbers and the Greek text.

11. Passages in lyric meters that were originally meant to be sung are
printed in italics to distinguish them from lines that were spoken or chanted.

12. As a general rule, a tragic chorus's longer songs are divided into pairs
of metrically equivalent stanzas known as *strophes* and *antistrophes*.

OEDIPUS (emerging from the thicket
    with ANTIGONE):
Up here! I am he! It's by sound that I see— Anapests[13] (138–148)
    to speak in a figurative manner.

CHORUS:
Io![14]
His looks are alarming and so is his voice!

OEDIPUS:
Don't think that I'm some kind of outlaw, I pray.

CHORUS:
O Zeus our protector, who *is* this old man?

OEDIPUS:
A person whose fate's not entirely blest,
    gentlemen guarding this land,
for clearly I wouldn't go creeping around,
    guided by alien eyes
and anchored to people as little as she—
    big as I am—otherwise.

CHORUS:
Ah! Were you born with eyes so dim?   Antistrophe A (149–169)
If so, your life's been long and grim,
or so it would appear.

13. An *anapest* is a metrical foot consisting of two short syllables followed
by a long. The anapestic meter was traditionally associated with marching. I
believe that anapestic passages were chanted—that is, pronounced with
emphatic rhythm—but not sung to a melody.

14. *Io* is an interjection expressing a sudden emotion, either good or bad,
like English "oh!" Pronounced "eeoo!"

And yet we can't permit you thus
to place a dreadful curse on us.
You've gone beyond the pale.

Lest you disturb that silent glen
where waters from a crater blend
with drafts of honey, leave!

All-hapless wanderer, beware!
Depart! Go far away from there.
O weary vagrant, leave!

If you have got some words to share,
then leave the glen and go to where
all have the right to speak.

OEDIPUS:
My daughter, which way should my
       thinking incline?   Anapests (170–175)

ANTIGONE:
    O father, respect their demands.
Give way and obey since we must.

OEDIPUS:
                     Very well.
   Then please take my hand.

ANTIGONE:
             It is done.

OEDIPUS:
I'm trusting you, strangers, and leaving this spot.
   Don't treat me unjustly for that.

CHORUS:
Old man, you won't be forced against   Strophe B (176–187)
*   your will to leave our land.*

OEDIPUS:
Still farther?

CHORUS:
*   Yes! Since you can see,*
young lady, lend a hand.

ANTIGONE:
Come where I lead you, father dear,
*   direct your limbs by mine*

————

————15

CHORUS:
A stranger in a foreign land,
*   must learn to hate and fear*
that which offends the city and
*   to love what it holds dear.*

OEDIPUS:
Keep leading me, daughter, until we have come Anapests (188–191)
    to where it's permitted to stand.
I wish to keep speaking and hear what is said
    but not break the laws of the land.

15. The meter shows that three short lines of the original Greek have been lost at this point. In my translation, they correspond to the seventh and eighth lines in Antistrophe B (starting at line 192).

CHORUS:
That's far enough! Don't step beyond   Antistrophe B (192–206)
   the marble platform there.

OEDIPUS:
Like so?

CHORUS:
      That's right.

OEDIPUS:
               And may I sit?

CHORUS:
Yes, make that rock your chair.

ANTIGONE:
It's up to me to help. Be calm.
   Go step by step with me.

OEDIPUS:
Sad ruin!

ANTIGONE:
      Share your ancient weight.
I'll hold it lovingly.

   (With ANTIGONE's help, OEDIPUS sits down on a
   second large rock.)

CHORUS:
Since now you've put yourself at ease,
   say who you are, poor man,
and why you suffer as you do,
   and where's your fatherland.

OEDIPUS:
I'm cityless. Now please refrain.   Lyric verses (207–253)

CHORUS:
Refrain from doing what? Explain!

OEDIPUS:
Don't ask me who I am!
  Don't question me in any way!

CHORUS:
Why not?

OEDIPUS:
    A horrid fate.

CHORUS:
Do tell!

OEDIPUS:
    O daughter, what to say?

CHORUS:
Reveal your origins, stranger—
  your father's, anyhow!

OEDIPUS:
Ah me! Alas! My daughter,
  what must I suffer now?

CHORUS:
Just speak! You've reached the border.
  You cannot step aside.

OEDIPUS:
I'll do so, since I haven't
any place to hide.

CHORUS:
And yet you still malinger!
Why must you be so slow?

OEDIPUS:
You've heard about a certain
. . . child of Laius?

CHORUS:
Whoa!

OEDIPUS:
You've also heard about the
Labdacid family
and Oedipus the wretched?

CHORUS:
O Zeus! Could you be he?
Oh! Oh!

OEDIPUS:
Don't be alarmed. It's only fate!
My daughter, what will happen now?

CHORUS:
Depart our land! Evacuate!

OEDIPUS:
But what about your recent vow?

CHORUS:
The gods don't punish people for
*   avenging injuries.*
The lies that counterbalance lies
*   are not designed to please.*
So you must leave the country now,
*   and do so on the run!*
Do not oppress my city with
*   the weight of what you've done.*

ANTIGONE:
Dear open-hearted strangers, since you've spurned
my ancient, sightless father, having learned
the things he did unwillingly, by fate,
at least feel pity, seeing my sorry state.
I come before you now to speak for him
and see you too. My eyes are not so dim.
Pretend I'm one of you and let him find,
for all his sins, that you can still be kind.
Our only chance is you. You're like a god.
Exceed our hopes! You only need to nod.
By child or wife, religion, property—
whatever you hold dear—I make this plea.
Conduct a search; you'll find no mortal who
escapes the end the gods would drive him to.

CHORAL LEADER:
Daughter of Oedipus, you needn't doubt
that your misfortunes rouse our sympathy,
but fear of gods' displeasure limits us;
we cannot change what we've already said.

OEDIPUS:
What good does reputation do or fame,
however fair, that simply drifts away?

So what if people say that Athens is   260
most reverent, that she and only she
protects the lives of persecuted men.
Where did that virtue go when I arrived?
You raised me up and now you banish me,
fearing my name and only that. It's not
my body that you fear, or deeds. My "deeds"
indeed are passive sufferings. The things
my parents did, if I may speak of them,
are really why you fear me so. Of that
I'm sure. Do they make me an evil man?   270
My crimes were self-defense, so even had
I acted knowingly, I couldn't be
condemned. I ventured forth in ignorance
when those by whose designs I suffered once
tried killing me again.[16] I beg you, please!
You made me leave that sanctuary. Save
my life! Don't treat the gods you honor so
as though they had no power. Recognize
that they keep watch on men, on pious men
and godless sinners equally, and for   280
the latter no escape has yet been found.
Be on their side. Don't darken Athens' bright
repute by sanctioning dishonest acts.
I am the suppliant you promised you'd
protect. Deliver me from danger now.
Don't scorn me, shocked by my disfigured face.
I am, in fact, a pious holy man
who brings you townsmen here good luck, and when

16. Literally: "Now knowing nothing, I came to where I came and was
being killed by those by whose knowing actions I suffered." This is Oedipus'
very condensed way of saying that when he neared Thebes in all innocence,
there was an attempt on his life by his father, who, with his mother, had
knowingly exposed him as an infant on Mount Citheron.

your lord, whoever leads you, does arrive,
you'll hear my story, learning everything.   290
Refrain from acting wickedly till then.

CHORAL LEADER:
Your arguments have shaken me, I must
admit, old sir. Your protestation had
no lack of weighty words. I think it best
to let our ruler sort these matters out.

OEDIPUS:
So be it! Where's the country's ruler now?

CHORAL LEADER:
He's visiting our land's ancestral seat.
The guard who summoned me has gone for him.

OEDIPUS:
Do you suppose he'll take an interest in
this sightless man and come to us himself?   300

CHORAL LEADER:
Yes, absolutely, once he hears your name.

OEDIPUS:
How will that information reach his ears?[17]

CHORAL LEADER:
The road is long, and travelers like to talk
of many things. Be brave, for once he hears
the gossip, he'll set forth. Your name, old sir,

---

17. A good question. Obviously, there is no plausible way for Theseus to
hear that Oedipus has arrived in Colonus, since the fact has just been revealed
to the chorus in the otherwise empty countryside.

looms large in every land. Perhaps he naps.
He'll hurry here when he's aware of you.

OEDIPUS:
If so, he'll bless his city, not just me.
What noble man is not his own best friend?

ANTIGONE:
O Zeus! I'm dumbstruck! Tell me what to think!   310

OEDIPUS:
What's startled you, Antigone?

ANTIGONE:
                                        I see
a woman drawing near. She rides a colt,
Sicilian, but her cap's from Thessaly.
The shadow cast by it conceals her face.
What should I say?
Is it or isn't it or am I mad?
It is! It isn't! I'm incapable
of speech! No, wait!

            (Enter ISMENE.)

It's not some other girl. Her brilliant eyes
saluting me as she approaches prove   320
that it's Ismene! No one else but she!

OEDIPUS:
What's that, my child?

ANTIGONE:
                        I see my sister's here.
Your daughter. Soon you'll recognize her voice.

ISMENE:
Father and sister, titles I employ
most happily, locating you was hard,
and now I scarcely see you through my tears.

OEDIPUS:
My child, you're here!

ISMENE:
                    Ill-fated father dear!

OEDIPUS:
You've come!

ISMENE:
                    It cost me toil and trouble too.

OEDIPUS:
Embrace me, child!

ISMENE:
                    I'm touching both of you.

OEDIPUS:
My crop of sisters!

ISMENE:
                    Wretched sustenance!   330

OEDIPUS:
For her and me?

ISMENE:
                    And hapless me—all three.

OEDIPUS:
What brings you here?

ISMENE:
                    I'm watching out for you.

OEDIPUS:
And longing?

ISMENE:
            Yes, and being a herald too,
for I'm my only trusted servant now.

OEDIPUS:
But what about your brothers? Can't they help?

ISMENE:
They've gone wherever. Things are bad with them.

OEDIPUS:
It's obvious what's happened: they're transformed
into Egyptian gentlemen, those two.
The males are sedentary there. They work
the loom. The women are the ones who go   340
abroad and earn their family's daily bread.[18]
My daughters, those who should endure your toils
luxuriate at home like tender girls,
while you have shared my awful suffering
instead.

18. The improbable assertion that Egyptian men sit at home at the loom
while women attend to the market is taken from Herodotus (2.35), who adds
that Egyptian women stand to urinate while men sit.

(Placing his hand on ANTIGONE's head.)

Why she'd no sooner given up
her baby food and gained a bit of strength
than she became my fellow wanderer,
an old man's guide. How many times she's braved
the wilderness, all barefoot, starving, lost,
battered by drenching rain and scorching heat,   350
disdaining comforts that a home provides
to see her father adequately fed.

(Switching to ISMENE.)

And you, my child, made secret trips from Thebes
to bring your father all the oracles
that mentioned him. When he was driven out,
you made yourself his faithful guardian.
    But now, Ismene, what's the tale you bring
your father? What's the mission rousting you
from home? You haven't come with empty hands,
I'm sure. I fear you have alarming news.   360

ISMENE:
Dear father, I'll omit the narrative
of how I suffered searching out the place
you did your foraging. I'd rather not
go through those toils again by naming them.
I've come to speak instead of evils that
have now enveloped your ill-fated sons.
    They wished at first to keep the city free
of strife by letting Creon keep the throne
in view of that longstanding family curse
from which your tragic house cannot break free,   370
but now some god or evil impulse drives

that pair of thrice unhappy men to strive
for power. Each desires tyranny.
The youthful one, though less in age, possessed
his elder brother, Polyneices', throne,
and banished him beyond his fatherland.[19]
The story is that he has made his way,
a refugee, to hill-girt Argos, where
he gained a wife and fellow warriors
with whom he'll either seize Cadmeia's plain   380
or fail and raise its glory heaven high.
    Father, these facts are more than merely words.
They're awful truths and make me wonder when
the gods will finally pity your ordeals.

OEDIPUS:
Has something made you think they ever will
consider me and end my suffering?

ISMENE:
Yes, something has: some recent oracles.

OEDIPUS:
Which recent oracles? What's prophesied?

ISMENE:
That you'll be sought by Thebans while alive
and after death for their good fortune's sake.   390

OEDIPUS:
Their fortunes hang on such a man as me?

19. Ismene's account contradicts Oedipus' assertion that Polyneices
ruled Thebes at some point and was responsible for Oedipus' banishment.

ISMENE:
All Theban power rests with you, they say.

OEDIPUS:
So I'm the man when I no longer am?

ISMENE:
The gods destroy and later on exalt.

OEDIPUS:
Destroyed in youth, exalted old—how kind!

ISMENE:
Creon is coming here to deal with these
developments, and soon, not ages hence.

OEDIPUS:
What's his specific purpose? Tell me that.

ISMENE:
He wants your resting place to be near Thebes,
in its control—outside its borders, though.   400

OEDIPUS:
What can they gain by my being buried there?

ISMENE:
Your tomb's neglect would be an awful curse.

OEDIPUS:
That shouldn't take a god to figure out.

ISMENE:
That's why they want you resting near their land
and not far off, not dwelling all alone.

OEDIPUS:
But will they bury me in Theban soil?

ISMENE:
No, father, kindred bloodshed won't permit.

OEDIPUS:
If not, they'll never gain control of me.

ISMENE:
Then Thebes will have a heavy price to pay.

OEDIPUS:
And will some circumstance foreshadow that?   410

ISMENE:
Your wrath will find them standing near your grave.

OEDIPUS:
Where did you hear these revelations, child?

ISMENE:
The delegates who came from Delphi's hearth.

OEDIPUS:
And Phoebus spoke those words concerning me?

ISMENE:
So they proclaimed when back on Theban soil.

OEDIPUS:
Is either son of mine aware of this?

ISMENE:
Both equally and very well aware.

OEDIPUS:

Those monsters! Gaining tyranny means more
to them by far than any love of me.

ISMENE:

A painful truth, and yet we must endure.   420

OEDIPUS:

I pray the gods *don't* quench their fated strife!
Make me the final judge of their dispute,
the battle that they have in hand, for which
they're lifting spears against each other now.
With me in charge, the current king would not
retain the throne and scepter long, nor would
the exile ever enter Thebes again.
They saw their father shamefully expelled
and didn't lift a hand, but watched while he
was driven out, proclaimed a fugitive.   430

        You'll say that I requested banishment;
therefore the city just approved my wish.
Not so! The day in question, while my soul
was agitated, death was all I sought.
Yes, death by stoning seemed the sweetest fate,[20]
but none stepped forth to aid my passion then.
In time my anguish cooled. I realized
my rage had gotten out of hand, had gone
too far chastising innocent mistakes.
And that was when the city forced me out,   440

20. Oedipus' tendency to rewrite the past is evident here. At the end of
Oedipus Rex, he begs emphatically to be exiled (1432–1437). He once mentions
death by unspecified means as an acceptable alternative to being exiled (1410–
1412). He never says anything about stoning.

their king of many years, while they, my sons,
who could have helped their father, did not act.
They couldn't spare a word. And so I've roamed
the world, a refugee, a homeless tramp.
From these two little maidens, insofar
as nature gave them strength, I've gotten food
and shelter, all that's owed to family.
My sons, abandoning their sire, seek
scepters and thrones, unfettered tyranny.
I'll never be allied with either one,   450
and neither one will ever have the joy
of ruling Thebes. The oracles I've heard
from you and certain ancient prophecies
fulfilled at last by Phoebus make me sure.
Let Thebes send Creon forth to hunt me down—
or any influential citizen.
Provided you, my foreign hosts, and these
exalted goddesses, who rule your deme,
defend me, I will be your city's great
preserver, harassing my enemies.   460

CHORUS:
We think you're fit to pity, Oedipus.
Your daughters too, and since you've volunteered
to be this land's protector, I'm inclined
to offer you a bit of kind advice.

OEDIPUS:
Yes, be my guide, my dearest, I'll obey.

CHORUS:
The goddesses that you encountered first,
whose ground you trod—they need a cleansing rite.

OEDIPUS:
Then tell me what to do, my foreign friend!

CHORUS:
Collect libations first with holy hands
from where some fountain bubbles ceaselessly.   470

OEDIPUS:
Then once I've drawn the purest water, what?

CHORUS:
You'll find some mixing bowls, true works of art.
Place wreaths around their necks and double grips.

OEDIPUS:
With little twigs or woolen ribbon wreaths?

CHORUS:
Use only fleece of baby lambs fresh shorn.

OEDIPUS:
All right. And what's my further duty then?

CHORUS:
To pour libations, facing toward the dawn.

OEDIPUS:
Am I to use the urns you've spoken of?

CHORUS:
Yes, three of them, and empty out the last.

OEDIPUS:
That final vessel, what should it contain?   480

CHORUS:
Water and honey. Not a drop of wine.

OEDIPUS:
And once the leaf-dark earth receives these gifts?

CHORUS:
Deposit twenty-seven olive boughs
with both your hands, and utter prayers like these . . .

OEDIPUS:
I long to hear these most important words.

CHORUS (whispering the prayer):
"You're called the kindly goddesses. Consent
with kindly hearts to save a suppliant."
Thus you or someone else on your behalf
should pray, but whisper. Don't lift up your voice!
Then turn and sneak away. I'll boldly stand   490
beside you once you've done those holy acts,
but otherwise I'd tremble doing so.

OEDIPUS:
My daughters, did you hear our neighbors' words?

ANTIGONE:
We did. Now tell us what *our* duties are.

OEDIPUS:
I haven't got the strength to go myself.
My eyesight's gone as well. I'm doubly cursed.
So one of you had better do the work.
One soul who prays sincerely satisfies
the gods as well as countless worshipers.

Act quickly though, and don't abandon me.   500
My body's lost its strength. I can't so much
as crawl alone. I need a helping hand.

ISMENE:
I'll go complete the rites. One question, though.
Where should this ceremony be performed?

CHORAL LEADER:
Beyond that grove. Whatever you might need,
a local resident will help you find.

ISMENE:
I'll go. You stay and guard our father well,
Antigone. One mustn't call the work
we do for parents toil—although it is.

        (Exit ISMENE through the thicket.)

CHORUS:
To waken old evil's a terrible thing,   Strophe A (510–520)
    there's something I'd ask about, though.

OEDIPUS:
What's that?

CHORUS:
The wretched, apparently unending pain
    you suffer wherever you go.

OEDIPUS:
By friendship, I'm begging you not to expose
    the wounds that I'd rather not show.

CHORUS:
Your legend is spreading all over the world.
*   The truth of it's what we would know.*

OEDIPUS:
Ōmoi![21]

CHORUS:
Please do me this favor!

OEDIPUS:
Pheu! Pheu![22]

CHORUS:
Give in! It would only be fair.

OEDIPUS:
I suffered much evil and chose to endure,   Antistrophe A (521–534)
*   but evil was not what I chose.*

CHORUS:
How so?

OEDIPUS:
The city provided a wedding for me
*   from which my misfortune arose.*

21. *Ōmoi* and *Oimoi*, the most common interjections in Greek tragedy, express distress. "Ah me!" would be a reasonable translation.

22. *Pheu* is a Greek interjection expressing grief and anger. In reading aloud, I recommend pronouncing it as a disyllable, "phay-oo."

CHORUS:
I hear that you entered an infamous bed,
    your mother's, to add to your woes.

OEDIPUS:
Ōmoi! It is death to me—hearing such things.
    Our union resulted in those . . .

CHORUS:
Those what?

OEDIPUS:
Two girls, my twin curses.

CHORUS:
O Zeus!

OEDIPUS:
They bloomed from the womb that we shared.

CHORUS:
Those maidens, then they're your descendants? Strophe B (535–541)

OEDIPUS:
    My daughters and sisters in one.

CHORUS:
Io!

OEDIPUS:
    For the myriad evils
    from which I'm unable to run

CHORUS:
you're surely enduring . . .

OEDIPUS:

    exceptional pain!

CHORUS:
 You sinned.

OEDIPUS:

    No, I didn't!

CHORUS:

    Explain!

OEDIPUS:
I welcomed a gift I should not have,
 rewarding the good I had done.

CHORUS:
Poor man, you committed a murder.   Antistrophe B (542–548)

OEDIPUS:
 What is *it that you wish to learn?*

CHORUS:
You murdered your father?

OEDIPUS:

    You're hitting
each sickness I've suffered in turn!

CHORUS:
You murdered him, didn't you?

OEDIPUS:

    Yes, I did, but
 I have a defense.

CHORUS:
Really? What?

(Enter THESEUS.)

OEDIPUS:
I acted in ignorance, blinded.
I'm pure where the law is concerned.

CHORAL LEADER:
Look! Aegeus's son has joined us now.
Your message worked. Lord Theseus is here!   550

THESEUS:
I gathered who you were some time ago,
Laius's son, on hearing that your eyes
were bloody wrecks, and now the sight of you
on coming here has made me sure of it.
Your garb and mournful face are proof enough.
Ill-fated Oedipus, I pity you
and would inquire what you hope to gain
from me or Athens, since you've settled here,
you and the helper standing next to you.
Enlighten me. Don't fear you'll tell a tale   560
so horrible that I'll abandon you.
We've much in common. I was also raised
away from home, a solitary man
confronting countless dangers all alone.
I never turn my back on homeless men,
withholding aid from those in desperate need.
I know that I'm a human being and don't
control the future any more than you.

OEDIPUS:
In brief remarks, your noble nature's clear,

my lord, so there's no need for many words
from me. You state correctly who I am,
by whom I was begotten, whence I came.
It's only left for me to indicate
my needs, and then my oratory's done.

THESEUS:
Yes, that's exactly what I'd like to hear.

OEDIPUS:
I bring my battered body as a gift.
It isn't very much to look at, true,
but profits it will bring are more than fair.

THESEUS:
How so? What sort of profits come from it?

OEDIPUS:
You'll see—in time, but not the present time.   580

THESEUS:
When *will* the profits manifest themselves?

OEDIPUS:
Upon my death, if you will bury me.

THESEUS:
But that's a final service. What about
the rest. Have you forgotten? Don't you care?

OEDIPUS:
All other things are there implicitly.

THESEUS:
Still, what you're asking for—it's rather small.

OEDIPUS:
In fact, it isn't small. It means a fight.

THESEUS:
Between your sons and me, by any chance?

OEDIPUS:
Yes, they're intent on making me return.

THESEUS:
If so, then staying in exile isn't right.   590

OEDIPUS:
But when I wished to stay, they banished me.

THESEUS:
In times of trouble, anger's out of place.

OEDIPUS:
Don't counsel me until you've heard my case.

THESEUS:
Go on. I shouldn't speak in ignorance.

OEDIPUS:
Ah, Theseus, I've suffered dreadful wrongs!

THESEUS:
You mean your family's ancient accidents?

OEDIPUS:
No. All of Greece has heard that story now.

THESEUS:
Then what's this superhuman suffering?

OEDIPUS:
The children I begat have banished me
without the hope of ever coming back   600
because of being my father's murderer.

THESEUS:
Why summon you, if you must live apart?

OEDIPUS:
The word of god compels their current acts.

THESEUS:
So oracles have threatened them—but how?

OEDIPUS:
They shall be badly bloodied *here* some day.

THESEUS:
But why should we and they be violent foes?

OEDIPUS:
Dear Aegeus's child, the gods, and gods
alone, are free from death and growing old.
All other things fall prey to ruthless Time.
The earth decays and mighty men decay.   610
As honor dies, dishonor flourishes.
The airy sentiments that bind good friends
and allied cities are impermanent.
To some it happens soon, to others late.
The sweet turns bitter, then turns back to love.
In Thebes it may be pleasant weather now
for you, but Time's prolific womb gives birth
to many nights and many days, wherein
they shall discover some excuse for arms
to scatter solemn bonds of amity.   620

Then shall my frigid, buried corpse awake
to warm itself on drafts of steaming blood,
if Zeus is Zeus and lord Apollo true.
But secret truths don't make for pleasant talk.
I end where I began. Provided you
honor your promises, you'll never call
your Oedipus a useless immigrant—
unless, of course, the gods are tricking me.

CHORAL LEADER:
He's promised all along that he'd confer
great favors, those and more, upon our land.   630

THESEUS:
Who'd spurn the promised kindnesses of such
a man? He's from an allied state, a friend
in war. Our hearths are common property.
Then too he supplicates our native gods
and promises no little recompense.
I'd never spurn this holy person's gifts.
I'll let him settle here, a citizen.
If this is where it pleases him to stay,
you'll have the job of guarding him, or else
he'll follow me. The choice is his. Describe   640
your preference, Oedipus, and we'll comply.

OEDIPUS:
Confer your blessings, Zeus, on men like these!

THESEUS:
What's your desire, though? To come with me?

OEDIPUS:
If fate allowed. However, this is where . . .

THESEUS:
Where you'll do what? For I won't hinder you.

OEDIPUS:
Where I'll defeat the men who banished me!

THESEUS:
Your presence here is quite a favor, then!

OEDIPUS:
Provided you discharge your promises.

THESEUS:
Be confident! I'll never let you down.

OEDIPUS:
I needn't bind a man like you with oaths.   650

THESEUS:
You have my word. An oath is nothing more.

OEDIPUS:
But how will you perform?

THESEUS:
                              What worries you?

OEDIPUS:
Some men may come.

THESEUS:
                    These men will handle that.

OEDIPUS:
Be careful leaving.

THESEUS:

                 Please don't lecture me!

OEDIPUS:

But one must fear . . .

THESEUS:

                 I never fear a thing.

OEDIPUS:

You haven't heard their threats.

THESEUS:

               And yet I'm sure
no one will capture you against my will.
Most angry threats are merely empty words
and nothing more, just dire prophecies
that vanish (poof!) when sanity returns.   660
Perhaps some men have boldly talked about
removing you. The sea they face is wide
and not hospitable to little ships.
Why even mention my protection? You
should feel secure if Phoebus sent you here.
Besides, when I'm not present physically,
my name's enough to ward off any harm.

     (Exit THESEUS.)

CHORUS:

Horse country here, Colonus, where   Strophe A (668–680)
the finest farms on earth are found,
and nightingales who fill the air
with melodies abound

in dense coverts on wine-dark vines,
and fruitful twigs the god has blest.
No breezes blow, no sunlight shines,
no storms disturb their rest.

The Bacchanalian reveler
lord Dionysus tramps the sod,
while goddesses with him aver
they nursed the infant god.

The rainy skies nurse daffodils,   Antistrophe A (681–694)
the favorite crown since early days
of Maid and Mother.[23] *Crocus thrills*
the eye with golden rays.

Our springs keep flowing, tireless;
their pristine currents never wane.
The wandering streams of Cephisus[24]
inseminate the plain,

and neither Muses' choruses
nor golden Aphrodite stand
aloof from festivals in his
abundant bottomland.

There is a certain kind of plant   Strophe B (695–706)
that Asia has to do without.

23. The Maid and Mother are Persephone and Demeter, famously worshiped at Eleusis.

24. A small river originating in Mount Parnes, the northern border of Attica, and emptying into the Saronic Gulf. It lies west of Athens and Colonus. Its southern extension now flows under a major highway.

The mighty isle of Pelops can't
produce this wondrous sprout.[25]

It blossoms here, a native shoot,
unconquered terror to hostile arms,
the gray wet nurse, the olive fruit,
a plant that no one harms.

For neither youth nor people who
associate with age would try.
It's guarded by Athena's blue
and Zeus's watchful eye.[26]

Abundant praise is due this state   Antistrophe B (707–719)
because a mighty deity
has deigned to make our people great
in stallions, colts, and sea.

Yes, lord Poseidon, it is you
through whom we've earned the highest praise:
you brought the horse's bridle to
our streets and alleyways.

Also the well-made ocean oar
that fits the hand and lightly skids

25. The isle of Pelops is the Peloponnesus. It would be absurd to assert that olive trees do not grow at all in southern Greece or Asia Minor. The underlying claim is perhaps that the domestic olives grown in Attica are so superior to others that they are virtually a different fruit. In that there may have been a speck of truth.

26. In Attica, some olive trees were sacred, protected from harm by severe legal penalties and said to be under the protection of Zeus. The legend was that these trees were propagated from one that Athena had miraculously produced on the Acropolis when she first became the city's patron.

across the waves, an escort for
the fifty Nereids.[27]

ANTIGONE:
O land so often eulogized, the time   720
has come to prove those lustrous phrases true.

OEDIPUS:
What's happening, my daughter?

ANTIGONE:
                              Creon's near.
approaching rapidly and not alone.

OEDIPUS:
My dear kind elders, counselors, I pray
that you deliver my salvation now!

CHORAL LEADER:
Courage. Your safety's guaranteed. I may
be old and weak. My native land is not.

          (Enter CREON attended by soldiers.)

CREON:
Kind gentlemen, this nation's settlers,
I see a certain fear infect your eyes
because of my abrupt arrival here,   730
but there's no need for fear or ugly words.
I haven't come with threats of force. I'm old
and well aware I'm entering a city-state

---

27. The fifty daughters of Nereus, a sea god. They themselves are lovely
goddesses inhabiting the sea. The most famous is Thetis, Achilles' mother.

as powerful as any found in Greece.
No, I've been sent despite advancing age
to urge this man to follow me to Thebes.
I'm sent by more than one. My orders come
from all the citizens. By kinship, though,
I'm most obliged to make his sorrows mine.

    Poor Oedipus, consider what I say   740
and come back home, for all Cadmeia calls,
and rightly so, but most of all do I.
It's I who feel your awful suffering
the most. I'd be a villain otherwise.
I see your wretched, solitary life,
a wanderer in dire poverty,
with one attendant, this young woman who
I never thought would sink to such a depth
as that to which the poor girl's fallen now,
your personal attendant, keeping you   750
alive through beggary, unmarried still,
a prize for any passerby to pluck.
Will you pretend that's not an ugly stain
on you and me and our entire house?
We can't conceal what everybody sees,
but you could hide these matters, Oedipus.
By our paternal gods, return to your
paternal house and city. Bid farewell
to Athens. It's a worthy state, but more
respect is owed your ancient nurse, your home.   760

OEDIPUS:
What insolence! There's nothing righteous that
your twisted rhetoric would not distort.
Why try such tricks on me? To capture me
a second time in bonds of grief and pain?
When I was sick with self-inflicted wounds,

I yearned for lifelong banishment, that's true,
but you refused to sanction my request!
Then, when my rage and madness ran its course
and living life at home was oh so sweet,
you rudely thrust me out and barred the gate!   770
So much for sacred bonds of kinship then!
Now seeing this state and people treat me well,
you've set your mind on owning me again,
disguising hardened hate with gentle speech,
as though unwanted favors brought delight.

  Suppose you had an urgent need. Suppose
a man rebuffed your desperate pleas for help,
but when your need no longer pressed, he gave
the gift, when kindness seemed no longer kind.
Such charity brings hollow joy at best,   780
and what you offer me is similar,
fine words in sound; in substance, cruelty.

  Let me explain your evil tricks to them.
You're seeking me, though not to bring me home,
but to some border area. That way
your city might escape destruction here.
You'll fail, however, gaining this alone:
my vengeful spirit always dwelling there.
As for my sons, they shall inherit land
from me, but only what they need for graves.   790

  I have a better grasp of Theban things
than you, for I have better teachers: Zeus
and Zeus's son, Apollo, lord of light.

  Your lying mouth has made its presence felt
with its abundant rhetoric, but all
that talking does far greater harm than good.

  I know I'm not persuading you, so leave!
Respect our choice. We're doing well enough
for all our hardships, doing as we please.

CREON:
All things considered, who will suffer more   800
because of your decision, you or me?

OEDIPUS:
I get the greatest pleasure hearing your
eager attempts to use persuasion fail.

CREON:
Poor man! You've grown no crop of wisdom yet?
You stain the good repute of growing old.

OEDIPUS:
You've mastered clever speech. I never met
an honest man who always spoke so well.

CREON:
Good speaking differs from verbosity.

OEDIPUS:
As though your words were brief and useful too!

CREON:
There are no useful words for one like you.   810

OEDIPUS:
Depart! I also speak for them. Withdraw!
And don't leave spies in this, my destined home.

CREON:
I call these men, not you, to witness how
you speak to friends. If I should capture you . . .

OEDIPUS:
Despite my allies here? I'm not concerned.

CREON:
I think that you'll be sorry anyway.

OEDIPUS:
What sort of action lies behind that threat?

CREON:
You have a pair of daughters. One's been seized
and taken off. The other one is next.

OEDIPUS:
Oimoi!

CREON:
                You'll quickly master that refrain.   820

OEDIPUS:
You have my child?

CREON:
                And soon the other one!

OEDIPUS (addressing the CHORUS):
My friends, do something! Don't betray my trust,
but make this foul intruder leave this land!

CHORAL LEADER:
Yes, leave our country quickly, stranger! Go!
We find your past and present actions wrong.

CREON (addressing the soldiers escorting him):
You men, the time has come for action. Take
that maiden, using force if she resists.

> (CREON's men seize ANTIGONE, slowly forcing her
> offstage.)

ANTIGONE:
Oimoi! Which way to run? Can any god
or mortal help?

CHORAL LEADER:
            What's that you're doing, sir?

CREON:
Not touching *him*, but *she* belongs to me.   830

OEDIPUS:
Lords of the earth!

CHORAL LEADER:
            Your action's incorrect!

CREON:
Not so.

CHORAL LEADER:
      Why not?

CREON:
            I'm taking what is mine

> (During the choral song, CREON's soldiers leave the
> stage with ANTIGONE in the direction of Thebes. The
> CHORUS does not try to interfere with the armed men.

The CHORAL LEADER does, however, stand in the way
of CREON's departure.)

OEDIPUS:
O city!   Strophe (833–843)

CHORUS:
Set the maiden free!
You're going to start a violent row.

CREON:
Make way!

CHORUS:
            What you're attempting we
can simply not allow!

CREON:
Do harm to me, you'll be my city's foe!

OEDIPUS:
That's just what I predicted!

CHORUS:
                        Let her go!
And do so now!

CREON:
            The weak don't make the law.

CHORUS:
Let go, I say.

CREON:
            And I reply, Withdraw!

CHORUS:
Come forward, local men! Unite!
My city falls to foreign might.
Come forward now and join the fight.

ANTIGONE:
Help, foreign friends! They're dragging me away!   844

OEDIPUS:
Where are you, child?

ANTIGONE:
                    I'm carried off by force!

OEDIPUS:
Give me your hands!

ANTIGONE:
                    I haven't got the strength!

CREON (to his attendants):
What are you waiting for?

OEDIPUS:
                    I'm lost, so lost!

        (Exit ANTIGONE with CREON's
        attendants.)

CREON:
You've lost a pair of walking sticks, that's true,
and yet you've won a certain victory

against your fatherland and friends, at whose   850
command I took these actions, "tyrant" though
I be. So savor victory. Some day
you'll realize that neither now nor then
have you been acting well, repulsing friends
and serving anger, ever your demise.

CHORAL LEADER:
Don't leave that spot!

CREON:
                    Hands off! I'm warning you!

CHORAL LEADER:
I won't release you after robbing us.

CREON:
Then quickly pay a greater price. Those two
won't be the only ones to feel my touch.

CHORAL LEADER:
What's your intention?

CREON:
                    Simple! Seizing *him*!   860

CHORAL LEADER:
Bold words!

CREON (sarcastically):
                    The deed's already good as done,
unless the country's ruler interferes.

OEDIPUS:
Have you no shame to threaten touching me?

CREON:
Oh, quiet down!

OEDIPUS:
          No! Let the spirits here
no longer check the curse that's on my lips
for you, you monster, who by force removed
my one surviving dearly cherished eye.
May Helios, the god of perfect sight,
therefore, make you and your entire clan
endure a life like mine while growing old.   870

CREON:
Are you observing this, you local men?

OEDIPUS:
They're watching you and me and note that I
respond by means of words to hostile deeds.

CREON:
I'll stand no more of this. I'm seizing him
myself, alone, despite my aging limbs.

      (During this song, CREON tries to drag OEDIPUS off-
      stage, but does not get far.)

OEDIPUS:
Help! Help!   Antistrophe (876–886)

CHORUS:
      What boldness you display
if this is what you hope to do.

CREON:
It is!

CHORUS:
If you succeed, I'll say
the city's fallen too.

CREON:
When justice helps, the weaker beat the strong.

OEDIPUS:
What words he spouts!

CHORUS:
He'll soon be proven wrong.

CREON:
That's your opinion. Zeus alone is sure.

CHORUS:
This is an outrage!

CREON:
One you must endure.

CHORUS:
Come quickly, you who rule the land,
with all the forces you command!
These men are getting out of hand!

(THESEUS enters, breathless, accompanied by a couple
of guards. CREON releases OEDIPUS.)

THESEUS:
What's the clamor? What's the crime? From fear of what do you

interrupt my sacrifice to him who rules the sea,
this Colonus's protector. Tell me everything!
Why have I come rushing here discomforting my feet?   890

OEDIPUS:
My dearest friend! I recognize your voice.
This person hurt me horribly just now!

THESEUS:
Which person did? And what's the injury?

OEDIPUS:
The man you see before you, Creon, seized
the only pair of daughters I possess.

THESEUS:
What's that?

OEDIPUS:
                    You've heard correctly how I'm wronged.

THESEUS:
Some servant—you! go back full-speed to where
the altar is and have the army, all
of it, both infantry and horsemen, stop
the sacrifices, ride with slackened reins   900
to where the merchants' double highways part,[28]

28. Theseus apparently intuits that the girls are being rushed out of
Colonus in the direction of Thebes, which lay to the west. Progress in that
direction was blocked by Mount Aegaleos. Evidently, the road leading out of
Colonus bifurcated at some point, with one branch going around Aegaleos'
northern edge, the other skirting it to the south. The southern route had to
merge at some point with the Sacred Way, the famous road from Athens to
Eleusis. Theseus wants his men to overtake the Thebans before they reach the

and save the maidens, lest this stranger laugh
at me for being overcome by force.
Get going!

(A servant rushes off.)

As for him, if I were ruled
by anger—which is what the man deserves—
he'd not escape my righteous fist unscarred.
Instead, we'll just apply his native laws.
There is no need for other ones.

(To CREON.)

Hear this!
Before you leave this country, you must place
those maidens here, right here, before my eyes.   910
In acting as you have, you've shown contempt
for me, your parents, friends, your native land.
You've burst upon a city that reveres
justice and never acts against the law,
then simply thrust authority aside,
deployed your force, and taken what you pleased.
You seem to think my city short of men,
a slaves' retreat, and me a weakling too.
I know it wasn't Thebes that ruined you.
That's not a place for breeding criminals.   920
They wouldn't praise your actions, learning how
you're robbing me of mine and robbing gods
by capturing defenseless suppliants.
I wouldn't cross *your* country's boundary lines,

---

fork in the road. At 1044–1064, however, the chorus assumes that the battle
will occur along the Sacred Way. Its actual location is never clarified; see note
38.

not if I had the world's most righteous cause,[29]
unless whoever ruled the land approved.
And loot and plunder? Never! I'm aware
of how a stranger ought to act abroad,
while you've disgraced the undeserving town
you call your own. Blame ever-passing time.   930
It's left you old and lost to common sense.
But now I must repeat my former words:
somebody better bring those children here
at once—unless you fancy life in chains,
our land's unwilling guest. Pay heed to what
I'm telling you. My mind and tongue are one.

CHORAL LEADER (to CREON):
You are a righteous man by lineage.
Your deeds, however, argue differently.

CREON:
I do not doubt this city's manliness
or its good counsel, son of Aegeus.   940
In doing what I did I just assumed
my kinsmen wouldn't spark such love in you
that you would shelter them against my will.
I thought you'd shun a filthy patricide,
one found accompanied by children whom
a foul and sacrilegious marriage bred.
I knew the prudent Areopagus,[30]
your nation's oldest court, did not allow

---

29. These lines sound like implicit criticism of Athenian imperialism
under the democracy, especially the assembly's authorization of the disastrous
invasion of Sicily.

30. The Areopagus, the "Hill of Ares," is near the Acropolis and gave its
name to an ancient judicial body that met there, consisting of former archons.
The powers of the Areopagus varied over the years. They were most famously

such tramps to dwell within your city's bounds;
and so I confidently seized my prey.   950
I wouldn't have, however, but he cast
a bitter curse on my offspring and me.
My sufferings demanded such revenge.
For anger's never old until the day
one dies. The dead escape its painful sting.
You'll do with me whatever pleases you.
Although I've spoken justly, I'm alone
and consequently weak. Yet even so,
I'll try some day to pay you fully back.

OEDIPUS:

What brazen insolence! For which is this   960
the more degrading, my old age or yours?
The words you spew of murders, marriages,
and misery name matters I endured
perforce. It pleased the deathless gods. Perhaps
they had an ancient grudge against my race.
You won't, however, find a fault in me
for which my self-destructive errors could be
considered punishment that I deserved.[31]

---

responsible for trying cases of homicide. Creon refers to the fact that the
Areopagus would execute or banish people guilty of homicide, not to mention
patricide.

31. Literally, "for, as for myself, you would not find against me any rebuke
for a mistake (*hamartia*) in retribution for which I committed these mistakes
against myself and my family." In a famous passage in the Poetics (1453a9–15),
Aristotle says that the ideal tragic hero's downfall comes about because of a
mistake (*hamartia*). The passage has led to an interminable debate on whether
Aristotle was thinking of a misstep caused by a moral failing or an innocent
intellectual mistake. Here Oedipus explicitly claims that there was no moral
failing on his part, no mistake for which he deserved punishment. Whether this
claim is justified is another question.

My father learned his fate from oracles:
his children's hands would bring about his death.   970
Explain your thought in blaming me for that!
My father hadn't sown me yet, nor had
my mother yet conceived me. I did not
exist! Once born, ill-fated as I was,
I came to fight my father, killing him.
I didn't know with whom I battled then.
Involuntary acts are free of blame.
And you've so little shame you make me speak
about my mother, being your sister too,
and so I shall. I won't be silent, since   980
your sacrilegious talk has gone so far.
She bore me, bore me, yes! She truly did!
But we'd no way of knowing that, so she
who bore me bore my children, bore her shame.
Yet this I know: you freely chose your foul,
abusive words. I didn't choose to wed
that way and only mention it when forced.
I can't be called an evil man because
of that unwilling wedding nor the death
for which you bitterly belabor me;   990
for answer just one simple question, please!
Suppose someone assaulted you right now
with deadly force, you righteous man, would you
ask him, "Are you my father, sir?" or fight?
Assuming that you're fond of life, you'd fight,
not cast about for legal precedents.
The gods were driving me along that path
of evils. Bring my father's soul to life.
Not even he will contradict my words,
but you're so lost to justice, you assume   1000
that everything's allowed in decent speech
and lay those charges out before these men.
You're very glad to flatter Theseus

and say how fairly governed Athens is.
Amid this adulation, you forget
that more than any city Athens knows
the way to honor gods. And that's the land
from which you'd steal this aging suppliant,
manhandle me, and take my daughters too!
I therefore beg these goddesses to hear   1010
my humble prayer, fulfill my urgent need,
and come as my defenders, teaching you
what kind of men this city's guarded by.

CHORAL LEADER:
Our guest's a worthy man. His injuries
are dire. He deserves protection, lord.

THESEUS:
We've chatted long enough. The criminals
are on the run. We're standing here abused.

CREON:
And what about your helpless prisoner?

THESEUS:
You lead the way. I'll follow you to where
you have the girls, assuming they're nearby,   1020
and you can show their hiding place—but if
your men are making off with them, we need
not hurry. Mine are in the hunt, so yours
will never get away to thank their gods.
Lead on! The captor's caught, as people say.
My fortune bagged a hunter—you. The prize
that's won by treachery is never safe.
And don't expect to find an ally now.
I know you couldn't reach your current pitch
of pride and daring all alone. There must   1030

have been accomplices you trusted in.[32]
That's something I'll investigate, or else
a single man might overthrow the state.
Does this make any sense to you or are
my words in vain—as warnings were before?

CREON:
I won't dispute your statements now, while here,
but back at home, we'll fashion some response.

THESEUS:
Fine threats! Keep walking, Creon. Oedipus,
stay here and ease your worried mind, for I
will never rest, so long as I'm alive,   1040
until I bring your children back to you.

> (Exeunt THESEUS and CREON.)

OEDIPUS:
God bless your noble nature, Theseus!
Your zealous care for us! Your righteousness!

CHORUS:
The enemy will wheel about.   Strophe A (1044–1058)
That's where I'd like to be.

32. There is no indication in the play that Creon had accomplices.
Oedipus makes a similar false assumption about the murder of Laius (OR
124–125). Perhaps Sophocles is commenting on a kind of paranoia prevalent
in the politics of his day, the tendency to see conspiracies everywhere. On the
other hand, Jebb says that the ancient Greek audience would have seen in
Theseus' suspicions "a proper level of wary sagacity" (*Sophocles: Plays, Oedipus
Coloneus*, 164).

They'll join the battle with a shout
near Pytho by the sea[33]

or on the gleaming torchlit strand
where goddesses reveal
their sacred rites to mortal man
and place a golden seal

on tongues of priests with whom they share
their rites, Eumolpidae,
their holy ministers.[34] *It's there*
or somewhere else nearby

that Theseus will soon display
his military powers.
We'll see the sisters safe today
within this land of ours.

Perhaps they've reached the pasture
      west   Antistrophe A (1059–1073)
of Oea's snowy hill[35]

33. Delphi, the site of Apollo's most famous temple, was also known as Pytho. "Pytho by the sea" refers to another temple of Apollo near the Bay of Eleusis. It was located on the Sacred Way, where a pass called Daphne facilitated crossing of the southern tip of Mount Aegaleos. The temple was demolished in antiquity, and a Byzantine monastery, still standing, was erected in its place.

34. The Eumolpidae were a family descended from the legendary Eumolpus, one of the early kings of Eleusis, to whom Demeter taught the secret rites practiced in her honor there. Members of the Eumolpidae clan were the high priests of Eleusinian mysteries and guardians of its secrets.

35. Here the chorus refers to the possibility that Creon's men took the northern route past Aegaleos. Oea was a deme that lay west of its northern tip.

on colts and chariots, possessed,
retreating with a will.

Creon will trip despite his flight.
The men Colonus bids
to capture him are full of fight,
as are the Theseids.[36]

Their bridles flash as they pass by,
and all the riders let
their reins go slack. The horses fly,
their headbands dripping sweat.

They pray to great Athena who
protects the cavalry
and praise the son of Rhea too,
the god who rules the sea.[37]

Hesitating now?
    Starting their attack?   Strophe B (1074–1084)
Soon I think we'll see
    sisters coming back,
sorely tried by kin
    dragging them away.
Zeus will make his strength
    manifest today.
Thus I prophesy
    noble victories.

36. The Theseids, literally "sons of Theseus," denote Theseus' men from the city, in contrast to the residents of Colonus, who were all or mostly horsemen.

37. Poseidon, son of Cronos and Rhea.

Oh to be a bird
  floating on the breeze!
a dove with churning wings
  passing to and fro,
gazing calmly on
  struggles down below!

Zeus who sees it all,   Antistrophe B (1085–1095)
  gods' almighty king,
grant our nation's chiefs
  strength for capturing
enemies by means of
  clever traps they've laid.
Pallas, Zeus's child,
  hear us, holy maid!
Phoebus, hunter god,
  sister standing near,
hunter of the swift,
  timid dappled deer,
we humbly pray that you
  come, immortal twins.
Guard our native land!
  Save our citizens!

CHORAL LEADER:
You can't complain, my wand'ring friend, that we   1096
are mediocre prophets, since I see
your girls and their companions coming back.

> (Enter ANTIGONE, ISMENE, THESEUS, and
> his attendants.)

OEDIPUS:
What do you mean? What? What!

ANTIGONE:

                                  O father dear!
I only wish some god would let you see   1100
the noble man who's brought us back to you!

OEDIPUS:
And both of you are here?

ANTIGONE:

                           The forceful hands
of Theseus's loyal friends made sure.

OEDIPUS:
Come to your father, daughter! Let me feel
your body, unexpectedly restored.

ANTIGONE:
You'll have your wish. We long to pleasure you.

OEDIPUS:
Where are you two?

ANTIGONE:

                    Together, drawing near.

OEDIPUS (embracing his daughters):
My dearest offspring!

ANTIGONE:

                    Every child is dear.

OEDIPUS (placing his hands on ANTIGONE's
      shoulders):
Man's staff.

ANTIGONE:
> Ill-fated staff, ill-fated man.

OEDIPUS:
My fondest wish comes true. Now death is not   1110
so horrible with you two standing by.
O daughters! Press yourselves against me. Let
our bodies intertwine. Thus I'll escape
my loneliness and wretched wandering.
Now tell me your adventures—briefly, though.
Few words suffice from children young as you.

ANTIGONE:
Our savior's present. Hear the tale from him.
He did the deed. I've nothing more to say.

OEDIPUS (addressing THESEUS):
Forgive this lengthy talk. I wished to greet
my children here, restored beyond all hope.   1120
I know my present joy in them is owed
to you alone, not any other man.
You saved them both. All credit goes to you.
So may the gods confer abundant gifts
on you and bless your nation, since I've found
that reason, piety, and honest speech
are cherished here as nowhere else on earth.
My words are based on knowledge. All I have
I owe to you alone of mortal men.
Give me your hand, my sovereign lord, to feel   1130
your touch and, if permitted, kiss your face.
But wait! How could a person cursed like me
ask you to touch a man whom every kind
of evil stains? I take it back. I won't
permit your touch. Only those with like

experience can truly share my pain.
So greet me standing where you are, and be
as just toward me in coming days as now.

THESEUS:
Neither your rather lengthy speech of joy
to these your children nor the fact that you   1140
would hear their voices first astonished me.
I didn't take offense at that at all.
My passion's not to gain a brighter fame
in people's talk than what my actions earn.
I've not been proven false in any vow
to you. I brought your daughters back alive,
unscathed by evils that had threatened them.
I needn't boast about my victory.
They'll tell you all the details later on,[38]
but I was given news just now, en route   1150
to here. I'd value your reaction, since
the message was remarkable, though brief.
One mustn't disregard the little things.

OEDIPUS:
What was the message, Theseus? Do tell.
I've no idea what you want to know.

THESEUS:
A man who's not a Theban citizen,
but is your kinsman, recently approached

---

38. Like Antigone (1117–1118), Theseus declines to describe the battle.
Apparently, Creon's men raced for the border after seizing the girls but were
run down by Athens' superior cavalry. If so, there is no logical way in which
either Theseus or Creon could have been directly involved in the action, since
they exited together on foot to look for the girls in Attica, long after Theseus
had dispatched the cavalry. See note 28.

Poseidon's altar. There he sits, where I
made sacrifice before being summoned here.

OEDIPUS:
But where's he from and what's he asking for?   1160

THESEUS:
I only know what I've been told: he seeks
a brief exchange of little weight with you.

OEDIPUS:
A supplication's always serious.

THESEUS:
He merely wants to have a talk with you
and then depart in safety, so they say.

OEDIPUS:
Who'd sit in supplication asking that?

THESEUS:
Have you some relative in Argos who
might ask a favor such as that from you?

OEDIPUS:
Stop there, my dearest!

THESEUS:
                                    What's the matter now?

OEDIPUS:
Don't ask my help!

THESEUS:
                              In what connection? Why?   1170

OEDIPUS:
From hearing you, I know the suppliant!

THESEUS:
Who is this undeserving person then?

OEDIPUS:
It's my detested son, my lord. To hear
his words would cause excruciating pain.

THESEUS:
But can't you listen, then refuse to grant
his wishes? Why is hearing him so hard?

OEDIPUS:
I hate the very sounds that leave his lips,
my lord. Don't pressure me to hear his suit.

THESEUS:
Are not we bound to honor suppliants?
Beware of disrespecting deities!   1180

ANTIGONE:
Young as I am, my father, heed my words!
Permit this man to take the action that
will ease his mind and also please the god.
Yes, let our brother join us sisters here.
Mere words, however inappropriate,
can't make a man abandon his beliefs.
Where is the harm in hearing what he says?
Speech, as a rule, exposes evil acts.
And you're his father. Thus it isn't right,
though he's offending you most heinously,   1190
to seek revenge by doing further wrong.

Have mercy! Other men have wicked sons
and hasty tempers. Still, their friends' advice
works like a magic spell to calm their souls.
Consider your misfortunes, not today's,
but those in which your parents were involved.
In contemplating them, I'm sure you'll see
that evil anger leads to evil ends.
In fact, there's rather cogent proof of that
in how your eyes' affliction came to be.   1200
You shouldn't make those seeking justice beg.
Give in! Being treated well yourself, do not
neglect the chance to pay the kindness back.

OEDIPUS:
Your satisfaction has a heavy price
for me, but let what pleases you occur.

(To THESEUS.)

I've one condition, lord. Suppose he comes,
make sure he doesn't overpower me.

THESEUS:
I need to hear your worries only once.
This isn't boasting: you'll be safe as long
as I by grace of heaven stay alive.   1210

(Exit THESEUS.)

CHORUS:
To me to crave too long a life,   Strophe (1211–1223)
despising any less,
clearly represents the height
of human foolishness.

Longevity piles up a store
of feelings close to pain,
and pleasure's gone forevermore;
one looks for it in vain.

If by chance a man survives
beyond the proper bounds,
a supervising guard arrives,
finishing his rounds.

For Hades' iron law, not chance,
binds everybody fast,
no lyres, choral hymns, or dance,
just death that comes at last.

Do not be born! I still maintain   Antistrophe (1224–1238)
that that's the finest plan,
or if you are, go whence you came
as quickly as you can.

Once you let the mindless bliss
of youthful days slip by,
sorrow's bludgeons never miss
and labors multiply.

Murder, envy, civil war,
strife and battles rage.
They're a person's lot before
the final step: old age.

Then lonely, powerless, afraid,
one sees no friendly face.
Every kind of evil's made
old age its dwelling place.

This wretch of a man's an example;
    my suffering isn't unique.

Epode (1239–1248)

He looks like a cape facing northward,
    a storm-weary surf-beaten peak,

battered from every direction.
    His weather is equally bleak.

For billows of terrible ruin
    prevent him from standing upright.

Some come from the region of sunset,
    and some from the roseate light.

      (Enter POLYNEICES.)

Some come from a southern direction,
    and some from the Scythian night.

ANTIGONE:
But look! It seems a stranger's joining us,
my father. Here he comes. He's all alone.   1250
He's spilling tears, and not just little drops.

OEDIPUS:
Who is it then?

ANTIGONE:
          We guessed correctly long
ago. It's Polyneices. Here he is.

POLYNEICES (to ANTIGONE and ISMENE):
Should I begin by shedding selfish tears

at griefs of mine, or weep at seeing his,
my ancient father's, ancient exiled king,
here in a foreign land with you and clothes
like these, these rags whose nauseating filth,
as ancient as the ancient man himself,
contaminates his flesh while breezes toss   1260
his unkempt hair above his eyeless head?
What scraps of nourishment he carries bear
a family resemblance to his clothes.
I hate myself for learning this so late.

(To OEDIPUS.)

Yes! I admit my heinous negligence
toward you. You won't need other witnesses.
But doesn't Mercy share the throne of Zeus
in all his actions? Won't you let her stand
by you? Offenses such as mine have cures,
while nothing I might do could make them worse.   1270

(He pauses.)

Why are you silent?
Say something, father! Speak! Don't turn away!
Give me some answer! Please don't make me leave
in silence, scorned, without explaining why!

(Turning toward ANTIGONE and ISMENE.)

I turn to you, his daughters, you who share
my blood, my sisters. Make our father move
his silent, resolutely hostile lips!
If not, I fear he'll spurn my humble plea,
despite the god, without a single word.

ANTIGONE:

Poor brother, tell him what you need yourself!   1280
It often happens that mere words arouse
such joy, disgust, or pity that a man,
however mute before, recovers speech.

POLYNEICES:

Well then, I'll try. That isn't bad advice.
My preface is: a god's protecting me.
This nation's ruler raised me up from where
I grasped his altar, giving me the right
to speak and listen, then to leave unharmed.
My hosts, I trust that you, my sisters here,
and father will accord those rights to me.   1290

    (Addressing OEDIPUS.)

Now, father, let me tell you why I came.
Our native land has banished me, cast out
because I sought your throne and absolute
authority as fits your eldest son.
Eteocles, though younger, balked at that.
He had me banished, not by logic, though,
or through some test like single combat. No!
He used persuasive speeches. I maintain
the curse that maddened you was most to blame
for his success, and prophets said the same.   1300
Making my way to Argos, I became
a son-in-law to King Adrastus. Then
I bound the leading men of Apia[39]
and its most famous warriors by oath.

39. Apia, another name for the Peloponnesus, is said to be derived from
the name of an early king of Argos, Apis.

My purpose was to launch a seven-pronged
attack on Thebes and either nobly die
or cleanse the land of those mistreating me.
But what's my goal in coming here, you ask?
Father, I come to you with humble prayers—
not mine alone, my loyal comrades' too,   1310
seven brigades of spearmen, who surround
the Theban plain in its entirety.
Amphiaráus marches there, being first
in hurling spears and first in augury.
The second, Tydeus the Oeneid,
is from Aetolia. An Argive's third,
Eteoclus. The fourth? His father, old
Taláus, sent Hippomedon. The fifth
is Capaneus, who boasts he'll level Thebes.
Parthenopaeus out of Arcady   1320
is sixth. His mother's lengthy maidenhood
explains his name: he's Atalanta's son.[40]
The seventh? Me, your son or else the spawn
of evil fate, but yours in name at least.
I lead the fearless Argive host to Thebes.
We all implore you by your daughters here
and by your life, requesting only this:
renounce the heavy wrath you feel toward me
as I set out to pay my brother back.
He banished me! He stole my fatherland!   1330
    Now if there's any truth in oracles,
they say the side you favor shall prevail.
By Theban fountains! Family deities!

40. Parthenopaeus' name is derived from *parthenos*, "virgin." His
mother was the famous runner Atalanta, who remained a virgin until a suitor,
Hippomenes, defeated her in a foot race (her prerequisite for marriage) by
dropping golden apples on the track, thus distracting her (Apollodorus
3.9.2).

I'm begging you to hear my plea and yield,
for I'm a homeless beggar just like you.
We live by flattering protectors, you
and I. Our fates are very much the same.
Meanwhile my brother runs the royal house
and dressed in fine apparel mocks us both.
If only you'd support my efforts, I'd   1340
destroy him easily in little time
and thus achieve your restoration, mine
as well, but first I'll throw the scoundrel out.
I'll boast of doing that if you consent.
There's no salvation otherwise for me.

CHORAL LEADER:
Respect his sponsor, Oedipus. Dispense
some fitting words and send him on his way.

OEDIPUS (to the CHORUS):
Guards of the local earth, if anyone
but Theseus had sent this person here,
believing he deserved an audience,   1350
he'd never hear my voice at all. As is,
his wish is granted: hear my words, he shall.
They're hardly ones to fill his life with cheer.

(To POLYNEICES.)

You evil creature! You'd the power once
your brother exercises now in Thebes.[41]

---

41. This statement is contradicted by Ismene's account of Theban affairs
(367–376), according to which the brothers at first yielded authority to Creon.
Only recently, well into the period of Oedipus' exile, did they both seek
power, and the upshot of their struggle was Polyneices' exile. There was no
period in which Polyneices ruled Thebes by himself or jointly with Eteocles.

That's when you drove your father out. It's thanks
to you I'm cityless and wearing rags
like these whose looks have made you sprinkle tears,
now that you're in such dire straits yourself.
Though I no longer weep, I never shall   1360
forget your homicidal treachery.
You are the reason I've befriended grief.
You banished me. Because of you I roam
and beg my daily bread from other men.
These maidens care for me. Had it been up
to you, I would have perished long ago.
Now they're my saviors; they're my nourishment.
They're men, not women, when there's work to do.
You two were born of someone else, not me.
Fate's yet to pay attention, but it shall,   1370
and soon. Your army may advance on Thebes,
but never topple it. That isn't possible.
Before that happens, you yourself will fall
in blood to keep your brother company.
I've let such curses loose on you before.[42]
I pray they fight with me as allies now
so you might honor your progenitors
and cease to treat your father scornfully
because he's blind. These females never did.
These curses shall defeat your royal hopes   1380

42. In earlier versions of Oedipus' legend, he remained in Thebes after
blinding himself and cursed his sons for various reasons. In the *Thebaid*, an
epic poem preserved in sparse fragments, he was evidently deranged and
cursed them for serving him with Cadmus' drinking cups and for sending
him the wrong cut of meat. Given Sophocles' version of events in *Oedipus
Rex*, we must assume that Oedipus cursed his sons initially for not intervening
when he was first driven into exile.

and prayers, if ancient laws are valid still
and Justice sits enthroned at Zeus's side.
　　I spit on you! I'm not your father! Leave,
you evil creature! Take the curses I've
called down on you. Don't gain your native land
by force of arms and don't come safely back
to hollow Argos! Die by kindred hands
and kill the selfsame man who's banished you!
　　Such are my curses. Now I call on hell
to make its hateful primal gloom your home.　　1390
I call on Ares, god who fills your minds
with hate. I call on nameless spirits here.
　　You've heard my words. Now going forth proclaim
to all Cadmean men and your brigades
of loyal comrades how lord Oedipus
distributes royal gifts among his sons.

CHORAL LEADER:
I haven't any sympathy for your
endeavors, Polyneices. Leave us now!

POLYNEICES:
My journey here, its poor success, my friends—
Oimoi! My sorrows mount. Is this the end　　1400
for which we marched from Argos? I'm undone!
I cannot tell my comrades what's occurred
or turn the expedition back. I must
confront my fate in silence, come what may.

　　　(Addressing ANTIGONE and ISMENE.)

You sisters, mine and his, his children too,
you've heard our father's curses raining down.

I've only one request. Assuming that
our father's curses work and somehow you
return to Thebes, don't fail to honor me.
Secure my burial and final rites. 1410
To praise you garner now for services
to him, another sort, no smaller, will
accrue for kindness such as that to me.

ANTIGONE:
O Polyneices, listen! Hear my words!

POLYNEICES:
What is it, dearest one, Antigone?

ANTIGONE:
Reverse directions! Lead the army back
to Argos! Don't destroy yourself and Thebes!

POLYNEICES:
Impossible! For after showing fear,
I couldn't ever lead my troops again.

ANTIGONE:
But why indulge in anger, brother? What's 1420
the benefit of overthrowing Thebes?

POLYNEICES:
Retreat is shameful. I'm the older one.
I can't endure my younger brother's taunts.

ANTIGONE:
But think! His prophecies are coming true!
He said you'd die at one another's hands!

POLYNEICES:
If that's his wish, we shouldn't disobey!

ANTIGONE:
I'm sick with grief! Who'll dare to follow you
after he hears our father's prophecies?

POLYNEICES:
I won't reveal them. Good commanders share
good news. They don't report the other kind.　　　　1430

ANTIGONE:
So then your mind is settled, brother dear?

POLYNEICES:
And don't try stopping me. I have to make
my journey now, though doomed to failure,
　　　　thanks
to father here and his Erinyes.
Zeus bless you both—provided you complete
my final rites. My life's beyond your help,
so let me go. Farewell! You'll never see
my living face again.

ANTIGONE:
　　　　　　　I'm sick with grief!

POLYNEICES:
Don't mourn for me.

ANTIGONE:
　　　　　　I'm watching you descend
with open eyes to death. Who wouldn't mourn?　　　1440

POLYNEICES:
It's fated.

ANTIGONE:
              No! Pay heed to me instead!

POLYNEICES:
Don't urge what cannot be.

ANTIGONE:
                        I can't go on,
deprived of you.

POLYNEICES:
              Whatever happens next
is in the hands of fate. I only pray
that you don't meet with evil. All men know
you don't deserve to suffer anymore.

        (Exit POLYNEICES.)

        (Thunder.)

CHORUS:
New evils from a novel source!   Strophe A (1447–1456)
    The sightless stranger is the cause—
unless perhaps it's destiny
    enforcing its unchanging laws.

I cannot argue that divine
    designs can ever go astray.
Time keeping watch destroys some things,
    restoring others in a day.

(Thunder.)

The heavens are rumbling! Zeus!

OEDIPUS:
My children, is there anybody near   1457
who'd bring most noble Theseus to me?

ANTIGONE:
What makes you want to summon him again?

OEDIPUS:
The winged thunderbolts of Zeus will soon   1460
be taking me to Hades! Hurry, please!

(Thunder.)

CHORUS:
The wondrous thunder hurled by
   Zeus,   Antistrophe A (1462–1471)
 ineffable, comes crashing down.
Stark fear has left my heart perplexed,
 invading me from foot to crown.

His lightning lights the sky once more.
 Will Zeus release his bolts? I fear
they never do set forth in vain.
 A sheer catastrophe is near.

(Thunder)

The heavens! Great heavens! O Zeus!

OEDIPUS:
My life's appointed end has come at last,   1472
my children. No escape is possible.

ANTIGONE:
What evidence convinces you of that?

OEDIPUS:
I simply know it well. Now someone, please!
go bring the country's leader here to me.

    (Thunder.)

CHORUS:
Once more the blasts of thunder ring   Strophe B (1477–1485)
across the sky for all they're worth.
O god, be gentle if you bring
some mystery to Mother Earth.

Be gracious when we meet, I pray!
Bestow a blessing greater than
the penalty that we must pay
for having seen this cursed man!

Zeus lord, I call on you!

OEDIPUS:
Where *is* he, children? Close at hand? Will I   1486
be breathing still and lucid when he comes?

ANTIGONE:
Why does your mental state concern you so?

OEDIPUS:
I want to pay his kindness back in full.
I promised that when I obtained his help.   1490

    (Thunder.)

CHORUS:
Come forth! Come forth! Step forward,
     son,   Antistrophe B (1491–1499)
no matter if you're far way
at the Poseidonion
sacrificing bulls today.

The stranger thinks it only fair
that you, your friends, and city be
compensated for the care
you've given him so graciously.

Make haste! O hurry, lord!

    (Enter THESEUS trailed by an attendant.)

THESEUS:
What's this collective clamor all about?   1500
It clearly emanates from you and him.
Was it a thunderbolt? A violent mix
of rain and hail? When god unleashes storms
like those, one never knows what they portend.

OEDIPUS:
How welcome your appearance is, my lord!
Some god contrived your timely presence here.

THESEUS:
Has something new come up, Laius's son?

OEDIPUS:
Life's pivot point. I didn't want to die
without fulfilling all my promises.

THESEUS:
What makes you think your end is drawing near?   1510

OEDIPUS:
The gods themselves play herald, making all
the signs predicted long ago appear.

THESEUS:
What are those aforementioned signs, old man?

OEDIPUS:
God's constant thunder! Countless lightning bolts
that fly from Zeus's undefeated hand!

THESEUS:
Enough. I know you've often prophesied
and never falsely. Tell me what to do.

OEDIPUS:
You'll learn about good fortune that awaits
your city, proof against the hurts of time.
I'll lead you where it's fated I must die—   1520
yes, lead you there without a guiding hand,
but you must not reveal this secret spot
or its vicinity to any man.
That way the place will always be your strength,
surpassing many shields and allied spears,

and once you've entered there yourself, alone,
you'll learn of sacred things, ineffable.
I won't say more with others present here
or even tell my children, whom I love,
and you must keep the secrets too, until   1530
you've lived your life. Then tell your noblest friend,
and he'll in turn select a worthy heir.
That way the spawn of Thebes will always leave
your homes unscathed, for many cities turn
unruly suddenly, despite good laws,
since gods, though sure, are slow to punish them
for madly disregarding piety.
Be careful you don't suffer that yourself,
but there's no need for me to lecture you!

    God's voice is calling now. The time has come   1540
to seek the place. No further lingering!

> (OEDIPUS moves slowly toward the grove. After a
> few steps, he turns to address his daughters. He is
> now able to see, even though his eyes have been
> destroyed.)

Come here, my daughters. I've become your guide.
Our former roles are wondrously reversed.
Yes, come along. You mustn't touch me, though,
but let me find my holy tomb myself,
my fated hiding place beneath the earth.
This way. Just follow me. Persephone
and Hermes, Hades' guide, direct my steps.

> (A few more steps. Then he turns to pray.)

    O light in darkness, light that once was mine,
my body touches you a final time!   1550

I'm creeping off to Hades now to end
my life in darkness.

> (A few more steps. Then he turns to address
> THESEUS.)

O my dearest friend!
may you yourself, your land and loyal men
be happy evermore and prosperous
and think of me, though dead, when fortune smiles.

> (Exeunt all into the grove. THESEUS' attendant exits
> last after hesitating.)

CHORUS:
You who rule the midnight throng,   Strophe (1556–1567)
lord Hades, if it isn't wrong
for me to name in prayerful song
Persephone and you,

I pray you let the stranger go
released from pain and cries of woe
and reach the barren plain below
where corpses lie concealed,

his Stygian abode, for he
has suffered undeservedly,
but now a just god should agree
to raise his spirit up.

Hear, goddesses of earth and great   Antistrophe (1568–1578)
unconquered beast who lies in wait,

lies snarling by the crowded gate,
Hades' bodyguard![43]

Death, son of Earth and Tartarus,
see that your dog makes way for this
our friend, who's on the precipice
of the underworld,

as he starts his journey toward
the nether plains in which the horde
of corpses dwell. Be kind, O lord
who grants eternal sleep.

(Enter ATTENDANT, emerging from the thicket.)

ATTENDANT:
Men! Citizens! I'd state the matter most
succinctly thus: Lord Oedipus is dead.   1580
I couldn't tell the tale of all the strange
events that happened there so briefly, though.

CHORAL LEADER:
The poor old man is really dead?

ATTENDANT:

                         At least
he's left his former, earthly life behind.

---

43. A reference to Cerberus, the three-headed dog at the entrance to the underworld.

CHORAL LEADER:
Poor man! By some divine and painless doom?

ATTENDANT:
Now there you touch the most amazing point.
You know, since you were present, how he made
his way from here. He didn't have a friend
as guide. He guided all of us himself.
He neared the steep descent with brazen steps   1590
that reach the underworld and stopped on one
of many crossing paths beside the bowl
once used for trading oaths by Pirithous[44]
and Theseus, eternal vows. Between
that and the jagged Thoricus,[45] he stopped,
sat on a marble tomb beside a tree,
a dead pear tree, and shed his filthy clothes.
He called his daughters, telling them to fetch
water for baths and prayer from nearby streams.
The girls ascended Green Demeter's hill,[46]   1600
which lay in view, and quickly did the things

44. A son of Zeus and king of a tribe known the Lapiths. He and Theseus vanquished the Centaurs when they disrupted Pirithous' wedding. Subsequently, Pirithous helped Theseus abduct the youthful Helen. Then he and Theseus entered the underworld, hoping to abduct Persephone as a wife for Pirithous. Pirithous was captured and imprisoned by Hades, but Theseus managed to escape. Sophocles' allusion (however minimal) to these bizarre, discreditable abduction tales is puzzling in view of his characterization of Theseus throughout the play.

45. Thoricus is the name of a hill and a deme some forty miles from Colonus. The name may be a scribal error, or else some other, forgotten Thoricus is meant.

46. The sanctuary of Green Demeter is one of the landmarks mentioned in the play that was not actually located in Colonus but in the area of the

their father told them to. They bathed him then
and gave him clothing fit for burial.
When he at last was fully satisfied,
when all that he commanded had been done,
the nether Zeus's thunder shook the earth.
His daughters panicked. Falling down around
their father's knees they sobbed unceasingly
with long, shrill wails and madly beat their breasts.
He hears their voices, sounding so distressed,   1610
gives them his hands and says, "My children, don't!
Today of days your father is no more.
All that I was has perished now, and you
have shed the heavy task of care for me.
I know how hard that was. A single word
will melt away those weary hardships, though.
No one will ever give you greater love
than what you had from me. In future days,
you'll have to carry on deprived of that."

They said such things embracing, all in tears,   1620
all sobbing violently, but finally reached
the end of that, and nothing more was heard.
Deep silence fell. Then suddenly a voice
burst forth, accosting him, and we were all
so frightened that our neck hairs stood erect.
A god was calling him from everywhere.
"O you there, Oedipus, what's causing this
delay? You've kept us waiting far too long!"
Perceiving that a god was calling him,

Areopagus and the Acropolis. It is mentioned by Aristophanes (*Lysistrata*
835). The women who have seized the Acropolis see a man hurrying up
the slope past it. Demeter is called "green" because of her association with
flourishing vegetation.

he summoned Theseus, the country's lord,   1630
and spoke to him as follows, "Dearest friend,
bestow the ancient pledge, your hand, upon
my girls. (You children, do the same for him.)
Promise you'll never hurt them willingly
but do whatever serves their interest best."
The noble Theseus held back his tears,
but promised under oath to do as asked.
When that was taken care of, Oedipus
caressed his girls with sightless hands and said:
"Have courage, children. Show your noble hearts.   1640
You must be going now. Don't ask to see
unlawful sights or hear forbidden words.
Leave quickly! Quickly! Theseus alone
is authorized to learn what happens next."

    The whole assembly heard him speak those words,
and so we trailed the maidens, leaving him
with further tears and moaning. Having walked
a little while, we turned around and lo!
the man was gone, had simply disappeared!
Our ruler held his hands before his face,   1650
shielding his eyes as though some dreadful act
he couldn't watch had just unfolded there.
A little later, we could see him pray
in silence, kiss the earth and raise his hands
hailing divine Olympus[47] all at once.

    Of Oedipus's death, no man could tell
what sort it was, excepting Theseus.
It wasn't any blazing bolt from god

---

47. Here Olympus stands for heaven. The actual mountain lies between
Thessaly and Macedonia.

or hurricane awakened on the sea
that ended Oedipus's life today.   1660
Some god escorted him, or else the dark
abode of dead souls opened graciously.
No weeping marked his passing. No disease
had tortured him. His death was wonderful
if ever mortal's was. For those who think
my story mad, I offer no defense.

CHORAL LEADER:
Where are his girls and their companions now?

ATTENDANT:
Not far away. They're coming here, as sounds
of wailing growing louder plainly show.

(Enter ANTIGONE and ISMENE.)

ANTIGONE:
Alas! For this ill-fated pair   Strophe A (1670–1696)
there's naught to do except lament
the doomed paternal blood we share,
for which we underwent

that unremitting servitude
in days gone by. Now at the end
we're left with what we felt and viewed
but cannot comprehend.

CHORAL LEADER:
What happened?

ANTIGONE:
        One can only speculate.

CHORAL LEADER:
Is he gone?

ANTIGONE:
He is and by the kind of death
    that anyone might crave—
not slain by Ares, god of war,
    nor drowned by ocean wave.

The plains of death invisible
    have taken him, and he
has gone to where he shall fulfill
    his secret destiny.

But O poor sister! deadly night
    descends on us, for how
can we on sea or land obtain
    our harsh subsistence now?

ISMENE:
We can't. O bloody Death take me!
    I hear my agéd father call.
I only wish to die with him.
    My future life's not life at all.

CHORUS:
O noblest pair of sisters, bear
what's sent by god with grace, and tame
your blazing hearts. Your fame is fair.
The path you've walked is free of blame.

ANTIGONE:
So one can long for what seemed bad,   Antistrophe A (1697–1723)
past suffering, and there are charms
in what was scorned, as when I had
my father in my arms.

O father, love, although you'll wear
the nether dark eternally,
you're not deprived, not even there,
of love from her and me.

CHORAL LEADER:
What's happened?

ANTIGONE:
He accomplished what he wished.

CHORAL LEADER:
What was that?

ANTIGONE:
He died inside a foreign land
as wished, and there he made
a resting place beneath the earth
in everlasting shade.

He left behind him mourners who
were overcome by grief.
I weep for you, my father dear,
but cannot find relief,

for sorrow great as mine. You died
  inside a foreign land,
as was your wish, but I could not
  be there to hold your hand.

ISMENE:
What fate awaits us, sister dear,
  now that our loving father's gone?

————————

  ————————48

CHORUS:
He ended life contentedly.
  His dreadful suffering is done.
Stop acting so distressed, my dears.
  Some evil touches everyone.

ANTIGONE:
O sister dear, let's turn around.   Strophe B (1724–1735)

ISMENE:
To do what?

ANTIGONE:
There's something that I long to see.

ISMENE:
What's that?

ANTIGONE:
A certain dwelling underground.

48. The meter shows that two lines have dropped out of the manuscript.

ISMENE:
Whose dwelling?

ANTIGONE:
Father's! Oh what misery!

ISMENE:
For us that's not a righteous act,
or don't you know . . .

ANTIGONE:
                    Why criticize?

ISMENE:
the truth? . . .

ANTIGONE:
                    Must you persist?

ISMENE:
                              In fact,
he fell concealed from human eyes.

ANTIGONE:
Yes, take me to that spot unknown
and cut me down.

ISMENE:
                    O grief and woe!
I'm powerless and all alone
and don't have anywhere to go.

CHORUS:
My friends, you've nothing more to dread.   Antistrophe B (1736–1750)

ANTIGONE:
Where to turn?

CHORUS:
You found a refuge formerly.

ANTIGONE:
From what?

CHORUS:
The evil fate from which you fled.

ANTIGONE:
I suppose.

CHORUS:
Then what can this new worry be?

ANTIGONE:
*I just don't know what I should do
to get back home.*

CHORUS:
                    Don't even try.

ANTIGONE:
There's trouble there.

CHORUS:
                    As always.

ANTIGONE:
                              True.
But now our troubles multiply.

(Enter THESEUS.)

CHORUS:
You face a mighty tide of woe.

ANTIGONE:
Indeed, I do.

CHORUS:
     Yes, I agree.

ANTIGONE:
Pheu! O Zeus, where should I go?
What is it fate intends for me?

THESEUS:
Stop weeping, my children. It isn't correct   Anapests (1751–1779)
to mourn in a case where the darkness below
brings comfort. The gods are resentful of that.

ANTIGONE:
Son Aegeus sired, we have a request.

THESEUS:
Yes? What is the service you'd have me perform?

ANTIGONE:
We'd see for ourselves where our father's interred.

THESEUS:
It's a secret location one may not approach.

ANTIGONE:
And what is the reason, Athenian lord?

THESEUS:

My children, your father forbade it himself.   1760
He said I should never go anywhere near
the gravesite and never show anyone where
the sacrosanct tomb of your father was found.
Provided I didn't, he said I would keep
my nation eternally happy and free.
I swore in the presence of god and of Oath,
the servant of Zeus who hears all, to obey.

ANTIGONE:

If those are the wishes my father expressed,
they must be respected. Now send us to Thebes,
primordial city. There might be a way   1770
that we can discourage the spilling of blood
that threatens our brothers.

THESEUS:

I'll do that and all of the services I
am capable of that will benefit you
and gratify him who is under the ground,
the newly departed. For me there's no rest.

CHORUS:

Now end your exchanges, and no longer try
to stir lamentation. In every respect,
these matters have ended as they were ordained.

Wisconsin Studies in Classics

Series Editors

Patricia A. Rosenmeyer, Laura McClure, and
Mark Stansbury-O'Donnell

Rudolf Blum
Hans H. Wellisch, translator
Kallimachos: The Alexandrian Library and the Origins of
Bibliography

David Castriota
Myth, Ethos, and Actuality: Official Art in Fifth Century B.C. Athens

Barbara Hughes Fowler, editor and translator
Archaic Greek Poetry: An Anthology

John H. Oakley and Rebecca H. Sinos
The Wedding in Ancient Athens

Richard Daniel De Puma and Jocelyn Penny Small, editors
Murlo and the Etruscans: Art and Society in Ancient Etruria

Judith Lynn Sebesta and Larissa Bonfante, editors
The World of Roman Costume

Jennifer Larson
Greek Heroine Cults

Warren G. Moon, editor
Polykleitos, the Doryphoros, and Tradition

Paul Plass
The Game of Death in Ancient Rome: Arena Sport and
Political Suicide

Margaret S. Drower
Flinders Petrie: A Life in Archaeology

Susan B. Matheson
Polygnotos and Vase Painting in Classical Athens

Jenifer Neils, editor
Worshipping Athena: Panathenaia and Parthenon

Sophocles
A verse translation by **David Mulroy,** with introduction and notes
Antigone

Geoffrey W. Bakewell
Aeschylus's "Suppliant Women": The Tragedy of Immigration

Elizabeth Paulette Baughan
Couched in Death: "Klinai" and Identity in Anatolia and Beyond

Benjamin Eldon Stevens
Silence in Catullus

Horace
Translated with commentary by **David R. Slavitt**
Odes

Martial
Translated with notes by **Susan McLean**
Selected Epigrams

Mary B. Hollinshead
Shaping Ceremony: Monumental Steps and Greek Architecture

Ovid
A verse translation by **Julia Dyson Hejduk,** with introduction and notes
The Offense of Love: "Ars Amatoria," "Remedia Amoris," and "Tristia" 2

Sophocles
A verse translation by **David Mulroy,** with introduction and notes
Oedipus at Colonus